Standing at the Edge
A Year of Days After Sudden Death

Standing at the Edge
A Year of Days After Sudden Death

By Meg Tipper

Apprentice House
Baltimore, Maryland

"This deeply personal and honest account of a mother's journey through grief is simultaneously unique and universal. It is one woman's story of traversing the waters of grief, attempting to make sense of her loss, intellectually, emotionally and spiritually, and yet it is a story we all share of the profundity of love and the heartbreak of loss which binds us together in our deepest humanity."

>Yeshe Richman Clarke, MSW, LGSW
>Bereavement Counselor, Contemplative Psychotherapist and co-founder of The Presence Project: www.presenceproject.net

"*Standing at the Edge* fiercely and lovingly tells a story of death, grief and love. Any mother, any daughter and every woman in recovery will be moved and changed by this book."

>Diane Cameron, syndicated columnist and author of *Out of the Woods* at Blogspot.com

"*Standing at the Edge*, a meditation in grief, reminds us of the utter centrality of honesty and gratitude, and introduces us to a woman who embodies them both. From intimate moments in which we delight in seeing her daughter Maggie, to the enlightened articulation of courageous faith, Meg Tipper gently draws us through her daily acts of devotional survival to a memoir of intellect and light."

>Nancy Jay Crumbine, Ph.D., Unitarian Universalist minister, professor at Dartmouth College, and author of the book, *Humility, Anger, and Grace: Meditations Towards a Life that Matters* at northboundbooks.com

"An unflinching look inside the experience of losing a child to epilepsy. Both interesting and helpful to neurologists who care for these families and to those who are grieving."

>Eric H. W. Kossoff, M.D., Associate Professor, Neurology and Pediatrics, Johns Hopkins Hospital

Copyright © 2010 by Meg Tipper

All rights reserved. No part of this book may be reproduced or transmitted in any form or by any means, electronic or mechanical, including photocopy, recording, or any information storage and retrieval system, without prior permission from the publisher (except by reviewers who may quote brief passages).

Photo Credits:
   Cover photo: Meg Tipper
   Author photo: Jim Himel

About the cover photo:
   I took the photograph the summer before Maggie died, when we were visiting my friend Margaret Kirk on the coast of Cornwall, England. Maggie and I had set off on a very hot day for a coastal walk, but early in the walk, Maggie stopped under a tree, breathing hard, dripping with sweat, and said, "I need a break." We stood in the shade, drank some water, and rested. Maggie had been having seizures, she was taking heavy duty medications, she was not at her best. I suggested we turn back, but before we did, I took my daughter's picture as she looked out at the walk we might have taken on a different day, under different circumstances.

·

ISBN: 978-1-934074-55-8 / 1-934074-54-3

Printed in the United States of America

First Edition

Published by Apprentice House
The Future of Publishing…Today!

Apprentice House
Communication Department
Loyola University in Maryland
4501 N. Charles Street
Baltimore, MD 21210
410.617.5265
410.617.5040 (fax)
www.ApprenticeHouse.com
info@ApprenticeHouse.com

To Maggie
for her extraordinary life,
and to everyone who carried me
after her death.

All of the proceeds from the sale of this book
will be donated to the Maggie Feiss Fund of the
Baltimore Community Foundation.

To find out more about the fund or to give
directly, go to www.bcf.org/feissm

The website for this book can be found at www.standingattheedge.org

Acknowledgments

Often after Maggie died, people would ask, "Are you writing?" And when I said yes, they would nod and say, "Good." Then, as publishing the book became a reality, people were similarly positive, leading me to believe that the book could be helpful not just to me but to others. I want to thank everyone who encouraged this process at every point along the way; that you believed in my words and their power to help heal grief and to honor Maggie's life was a great blessing.

There are some people who deserve acknowledgment for their particular contributions to the book:

Robbie McHardy, who was my first reader and urged me on

Eric Kossoff for attending to my medical questions and for his blurb

Kirt Kempter for matters geological

Mary Carol for help with getting the book proposal to speak directly

Lucy Hoopes for encouragement and guidance to connect with Apprentice House

Kevin Atticks for bringing me into the Apprentice House fold and for his patience with his "most attentive" writer

Jennifer Minnich for sharing the vision, endless attention to detail and knowing the right cover photo before I did

Bill Tipper for collecting many of the photographs

Bob Feroli for his wizardry with photo software and his patience and perfectionism

Clare Petersberger for just the right words, time and time again, most recently with my title

Diane Cameron for the advice to hold nothing back and for astute editing, especially of content

Anita Sherman for attention to the details, especially the nuances of language, and for her tears

Yeshe Clarke for saying yes to a stranger and for wanting to read every word

Nancy Grumbine for seeing my words as meditations and for getting the perfect blurb written before dinner

Rafael Alvarez for advice about the writing biz and for popping up when I need him

Stephanie Helline and Amy Goodwin; side by side, each has tight hold of my hand for the marketing journey

Jim for the time, space and safety to grieve and to write and publish a book along side all the other blessings of our lives and love

Introduction

This story begins with an ending: my daughter, Maggie's, death on November 2, 2008. She was twenty-two. In order to put her death and my life afterwards into context, here is some background.

I married my high school and college sweetheart, Bill Feiss. We had a son, Stephen, and five years later, a daughter, Maggie. We had a lovely little house with a big yard in Lutherville, Maryland, north of Baltimore, where both our extended families lived. It was a great neighborhood, with lots of kids. We had good friends and interesting careers, we took nice vacations. We had two cars in the driveway; we even had a very well behaved chocolate Labrador retriever. Our marriage was not perfect; there were lots of rocky times, but we were living a good life, if not the dream.

In December of 1997, when she was eleven, Maggie had her first seizure while Christmas shopping with her Dad. She fell down with convulsions and was taken by ambulance to the hospital; it was terrifying. Tests of her brain revealed the electrical patterns associated with chronic seizures, and as we began to learn more about the signs of seizures, we realized that Maggie had been having them in different forms for quite some time. She was diagnosed with epilepsy.

While it was terribly difficult to accept that our very vibrant Maggie had a life threatening illness, we were fortunate: Maggie's seizures responded well to medication; she took her diagnosis in stride and lived her life very independently and fully. For her sophomore year of high school, Maggie and I lived in York, England, while I was on sabbatical from my teaching job. Later, she got her driver's license, became an intrepid world traveler, acted in plays, did extensive community service, was active in our church, and had a host of friends of all ages. We had every reason to hope that Maggie would be one of the lucky ones: someone with epilepsy who could lead a very normal life.

There were always periodic seizures, terrible, crippling attacks that left her disoriented, exhausted, and often bruised or scraped. There were side effects of the medications: fatigue, weight gain, slower mental processing and some memory loss. There were consequences for us who loved her: always the fear of seizures, of her seizing in an unsafe place, of a seizure that wouldn't stop. We worried that Maggie pushed herself so hard and was not always good about remembering to take her medications. We had to make hard decisions about what she could do and how much we needed to tell people she was with.

Another terrible blow to our family occurred in 2004 when Bill and I separated. Stephen was away at college and therefore was more buffered from the impact; plus he had seen it coming. Maggie was in her senior year of high school, still living at home, and had been largely unaware of the difficulties that had gnawed at her parents' marriage. The separation was difficult for all of us, but especially for Maggie.

Maggie graduated from Bryn Mawr School in Baltimore and charged off to the University of Southern California (USC) to major in Policy, Planning and Development. She always said she wanted to come back and "fix Baltimore." In college, the seizures began to get worse, but Maggie still carried a full course load, organized major fund raisers for the American Cancer Society, played Ultimate Frisbee, and had a huge network of friends. However, her disease was taking its toll: she could no longer drive; she began the endless rounds of different combinations of epilepsy medications, some of which severely impaired her thinking, and she began to have to limit some of her activities. Still, there was never a question that she would travel for a semester of her junior year, and she chose a program of studying the arts and culture of Ghana. She loved that experience and even bought a goat for a shaman to use in healing her epilepsy!

Maggie graduated in four years from USC in June, 2008. She had intended to take off on a world tour after graduation, but she had begun having seizures in clusters, one after another, and the medications she was taking were too debilitating for her to travel alone. She came home. At the time, it was a disappointment for all of us. Now, those five months with her feel like the greatest gift. On November 2, 2008, Maggie died suddenly. The cause of death was SUDEP, an acronym standing for sudden, unexplained death in epilepsy patients.

At Maggie's memorial service, our minister, Clare Petersberger adapted the following introduction from words Adlai Stevenson spoke at the memorial service for Eleanor Roosevelt in 1962: "Our hearts begin to heal as we give sorrow words. For we are always saying farewell in this world, always standing at the edge of a loss attempting to retrieve some human meaning from the silence."

Almost immediately after Maggie died, I began writing. It was my way to keep from falling over the edge.

"He put an arm around me. 'I know,' he said. 'I know.'

He didn't really know, of course. Not really. And yet that was what he said, and I was soothed to hear it. For I knew what he meant. We all have our sorrows, and although the exact delineaments, weight and dimensions of grief are different for everyone, the color of grief is common to us all. 'I know,' he said, because he was human, and therefore, in a way, he did." (Setterfield 388-9)

November 2

The Corpse
My daughter lay dead upstairs in her father's house, in his bed. Amid the total shock of this fact, I knew I needed to be with her body. I didn't need to see her; I needed to feel her hair in my hands. This act has been so much a part of my mothering, from her first moments at my breast to all acts of comfort and affection over the twenty-two years of her life; I needed this gesture to say good-bye. When I entered the room, I only glanced at her face, seeing quickly that there was no life left, that she was completely and utterly gone from this shell, already hardening. I slid my fingers into the tangle of her hair but I couldn't linger; it was too unimaginably painful.

No Man's Land
I had this strange feeling when it was just my ex-husband Bill, Bill's brother Chris, my boyfriend Jim, and I who knew of Maggie's death. Maggie was still alive to everyone else who knew her. Maybe if we just didn't tell anyone, we could keep her alive. If no one else knew, then it wouldn't be true.

Standing at the Edge

November 3

No. No. No.

Last night, Bill was standing at the door of his house as I arrived, having been summoned by his desperate phone call to come at once. Part of me knew. I reasoned on the way downtown: in a medical emergency, I would be driving to the hospital. As I rounded the corner of his street, I saw the police car in front of his house and thought *something is terribly wrong*, but how could my mind even allow itself the thought of my own child's death? Bill's face was tortured, and he croaked out in a pinched voice not at all his own, "Maggie died." All I remember is collapsing into his arms and moaning, "No. No. No," over and over again.

This morning, having slept little, Jim drove me to Bill's even before sun rise, so that Bill and I could call our son, Stephen, together. There was this black silence after we said the words; then he too said, "No."

Jim then took me out to Mom's. I put my arms around her little frame, so sorry to bring this sadness into her life. And at the news, she turned away from me, staggered into her living room, and moaned, just as I had done, "Oh. No. No. No."

Over and over again, as we limped through the nightmare

of delivering the news of Maggie's death, this was what we heard: the impossibility, the incomprehensibility, the NO.

In Some Ways, This is the Easy Part

My dear friends, Annie and Gregor, whose son Galen was murdered at the age of eighteen, dropped everything and drove down from Massachusetts to be with us. Annie told me, "In some ways, this is the easy part," and I knew immediately that it was true. Now, when the shock is powerful and I am being carried by people and prayer and the outpouring of love, this may be a coast compared to the Sisyphus life into which I will awaken.

November 4

Morning Walk
I woke up suddenly, very early, and immediately my mind was spinning. I was composing the obituary, running through logistics for establishing a memorial fund, remembering who else we needed to call. There would be no more sleeping.

I knew if I were to make it through this day, I needed to settle down and clear my mind, to feel calm enough for prayer. I hoped a walk might do it, so I set off in the dark for the trolley path, which I found littered with yellow maple leaves. As the sun rose, the leaves reflected the first light, and I found some peace. I wrote this haiku after I got home:

> Black path, edge of dawn
> Maple leaves scattered catch light
> I walk on the stars

The Funeral Home
Being in the funeral home was awful: the business of death clothed in an affected sympathy. There are so many ways in which to spend money on the dead, and making decisions about that felt easy but stupid. We went pretty

low budget and still signed over more than two thousand dollars. They had made the body up for viewing because Stephen had not seen Maggie, and we wanted him to have that option, which he decided to take. Bill went in with him; I stayed out. Later I second guessed myself, not because I needed to see Maggie's body again, but because I thought I should have been with Stephen. But when I confessed that to him, he said, "You were right there when we came out, Mom. It was fine." He amazes me.

Heightened Senses

People ask how I am. I have likened this to a drug trip. Lights are bright. Smells are strong (and usually unpleasant). Food tastes strange. I am hot; I am cold. Nothing is as it has always been in this land of shock from sudden death.

November 5

Blessing in Disguise

My brother Bill told me this story: just after I called and told him of Maggie's death, he tried to meditate but could not settle his mind. So, searching for some peace, he turned to a deck of "angel cards." He called upon his own and Maggie's guardian angels to guide his choice of a card to provide some understanding. The card he drew was "Blessing in Disguise."

While I am plenty skeptical about angel cards, I do see blessings everywhere. The greatest are the ways in which the rifts between Bill's and my families have dissolved. All of the blame, unfortunate but probably inevitable after divorce, is gone, melted by the pain of our common loss and our desire to help each other. At various times in this surreal week so many odd combinations of people have squeezed into Bill's little row house in Locust Point, where we all gathered to mourn: all the ex-in-laws, my boyfriend, Bill's girlfriend, old friends and neighbors, colleagues, friends of Maggie's. It was immediately clear that there was powerful love and immense blessing flowing from this unimaginable tragedy.

Meeting

For over twenty-three years, I have used a twelve step recovery program to cope with life. By genetics, nature and habit, my impulse is to escape, especially something painful. However, slowly, I have learned to stay with whatever life brings me and to learn from it. I even have learned to be grateful.

Today I returned to my home group meeting. I sat in the circle feeling a dichotomy: everything is upside down in the unfamiliar interior world into which I have been dropped, and, at the same time, there is peace and comfort in the ritual and familiarity of my meeting: the readings, the wisdom of the program, the love and prayer in the faces of people as they catch my eye. I took it in as much as I could, but I left before the closing prayer, unable to bear any personal attention.

November 6

Hair

Bill had the great wisdom to ask the funeral home to save four locks of Maggie's beautiful hair before they sent her body to be cremated. My brothers, Kendal, Bill, and Charlie, and I were sitting quietly in my brother Bill's living room, watching the leaves fall. I was drinking tea. I went and pulled the envelope from my purse. Margaret Oliver Feiss was typed on the front. The paper was still a bit damp from the lock of clean, wet hair they had snipped and sealed inside. I pulled my brothers in beside me on the couch and opened the envelope. One by one, we held the curl of dark, luscious hair, and we cried, quietly. Later in the day we took a walk together in the woods below my brother's house. The leaves were tumbling fast, making all of us very much aware that fall is the season of letting go.

Hugs

Everyone wants to hug me. Most of the time a hug feels good, but sometimes it doesn't: too much perfume, a really big person squeezes me too tight or a tall person bends me backwards and it hurts my lower back; sometimes glasses or buttons or a big necklace stick into me. But mostly, I like hugs because there really aren't any words that mean anything, and a hug says that. My favorite hug has been the one that breaks off but still holds on, pulls back to look into each other's eyes and then comes to rest with both foreheads touching, sort of a Klingon mind meld of grief.

Planning the Memorial Service

Bill, Stephen and I met with Clare Petersberger, our minister at the Unitarian Universalist Church in Towson, for the most surreal of all possible tasks: to plan the memorial service for Maggie. Clare is a pro, and she created a space in which to mourn together and also get down to business. We came out feeling good about our plans, a celebration of Maggie's extraordinary life and spirit.

We each have our jobs to do; one of mine is to provide the photos and text for the order of service. I knew I wanted a quotation for the cover and was searching poems and songs for the right one, when I remembered a condolence note from one of my former colleagues at Gilman, Ned Harris, which contained the poem "High Flight." I dug up the letter, reread the poem, and found the first two lines provided me with the message I was looking for:

> Oh! I have slipped the surly bonds of earth
> And danced the skies on laughter-silvered wings;
>
> > Pilot Officer Gillespie Magee
> > No 412 squadron, RCAF
> > *Killed 11 December 1941*

November 7

The Maggie Feiss Fund

There were several things that came to me the night Maggie died as I tried in vain to sleep. Among them was the idea of creating a memorial fund for Maggie at the Baltimore Community Foundation. Bill, Stephen, and I immediately began thinking and planning and working with BCF to make it happen. Today, the website went live and people can begin making contributions to the Maggie Feiss Fund. The URL is www.bcf.org/feissm. The blurb we wrote reads:

The fund is dedicated to help the causes which Maggie worked hard for and cared deeply about in her short but brilliant life: cancer research and care, urban renewal and development, public transportation, gay rights advocacy, educational opportunity, and diversity. In addition, we, her family, will add to the fund's purpose: support to people with epilepsy.

These are gifts in love and celebration of Maggie's spirit, energy, and impatience for change in a troubled world.

Another Dead Child

Several times, people have offered to connect me with

other people who have lost children. I know that there will come a time when I welcome such conversations and find them a comfort, but right now I am nowhere close to ready. I can't bear another person's pain, or loss, or sadness. I want to pull my loss close and share it with other people who knew and loved Maggie. One of the greatest comforts has been having Anne Marie and Gregor with us, who knew and loved Maggie and who also have lost their dear son, Galen. As Annie was leaving, I said, "Who could have imagined when we became friends freshman year at Skidmore College, that we would share such an unspeakable bond?" There is so much more in life than we can ever see.

Water

I want to drink water, glass after glass, all day. Sometimes I have very light herbal tea and honey. I also crave my bath and need it like a drug in order to sleep. Sometimes sinking down into that hot water is the only part of my day when I feel comfortable and safe. It is one time when I can cry.

November 8

The Obituary

I have been in the throes of speaking on the phone and writing notes for the newspaper for Maggie's obituary. I never really paid attention to the obituary as news item, which it must be. Here's how it works: the paper does not automatically run the obituary; you need to "sell" your loved one's death as newsworthy. If you want to be assured that people will learn of the death in the newspaper, you must pay for a death notice. I guess a young person's death has sufficient shock value to be desirable from an obituary editor's perspective, but is problematic because there isn't that much to write about. The editor asked me about Maggie's "hobbies," which just seemed absurd. As it was, the headline finally ran: Margaret Feiss, Enthusiastic Volunteer.

The Last

As early as the first night after Maggie's death, I began thinking over and over of the last time that we were together. It was Friday afternoon, Halloween. Bill and Maggie dropped by Jim's unexpectedly because Maggie wanted to look in the costume box. They had not eaten lunch, and so

I fixed some non-pasta noodles Maggie had told me about and which I had found at the Korean grocery store. I mixed in some home-made pesto, and both she and Bill devoured them. We were all delighted with this great new discovery for her very strict Ketogenic diet, which her neurologist had recommended she try in an effort to quell the seizures. It was a beautiful day; we sat outside to eat, on the porch at the picnic table. Bill stayed there and talked with Jim, while Maggie and I went to the basement to root through costumes. We remembered how she had dressed up for past Halloweens and fooled with some concoctions she might get together for this year. Nothing was decided, but she took a few different things.

As Bill and Maggie were getting ready to leave, I stood alongside the car. The top was down and the sun was shining on Maggie's hair. I remember thinking how beautiful she was. As Bill drove off, they both waved. It was such a simple but entirely perfect time.

I have dissected those final moments, trying to take a measure of how we left each other. It is silly that this last encounter should have so much more weight than all of the other times we spent together, and, I'm sure as time goes on, it will fall more into proportion. But initially, I have needed to cling to the nearness of this last time together.

November 9

Capacity for Feeling

I have been trying to articulate my feelings and realize how inadequate I am to the task. Not only are words insufficient, but I do not even recognize these strange combinations of feelings that occur simultaneously and that seem enlarged beyond all recognition. I can have overpowering sadness and loss running within this current of gratitude and love and amazement. The either/or dualities and absolutes, the names for emotions and moods, have completely imploded under the weight of this loss.

November 10

Shopping

Having cancelled our plans to go scuba diving in Bonaire, Jim and I decided it would be good to get away for a few days in Ocean City. On our way to the beach, we stopped off at the outlet stores in Queenstown. Neither one of us is much of a shopper, but we always like a bargain. I collected a few things to try on and headed for the dressing room. I closed the door behind me, hung the hangers on the hook inside the door, and suddenly had a huge lump in my throat. I was totally unprepared for the fact that the only time I really liked to shop was with Maggie, that we would get fitting rooms side by side and prance around outside to show off and get each other's opinion. I was so undone, I couldn't even try the clothes on, I just stood there sobbing and trying to collect myself, sure that I would never be able to shop for clothes again.

November 11

The Sea

I returned to the womb of the sea. I sat, staring out the window at the roll of the waves. I walked, just one foot in front of the other. Walked and walked and walked, with the sound of the surf and the cold wind on my face. I tried to make my mind blank: the expanse of the sand, of the horizon line, the drift of clouds, and it did feel quiet for awhile, some small peace. But always Maggie would return, like diving into cold water, the shock of her death.

November 12

You Can Do This Mom

Through these early days, I have felt Maggie so powerfully, like she has been working hard, having a hard time letting go. I was writing my eulogy, struggling; I read the draft out loud and was crying. I couldn't imagine reading it at her memorial service. Suddenly, I heard her voice so clearly, not just imagined, but real: "You can do this Mom."

Eulogy

The night of November 2 was the only one during which I could not sleep. Many things swirled through my mind. One thought was that I wanted everyone to dance at Maggie's funeral; the idea was connected to an experience she and I had recently. I ran this idea by several people and no one was really excited. Jim said, "I just don't want it to fall flat. I keep seeing all these old people standing there, feeling uncomfortable." But I felt strongly that it was what Maggie wanted; so I kept it.

Here is what I wrote for my eulogy:

I got a text message from Maggie on Saturday afternoon,

three weeks ago: "Dad can't go to Blues Traveler tonight, if you and Jim want to take me, the tickets are yours."

Maggie loved the concert from the first note; we kept meeting each other's eyes across the table and smiling while we sang along. She knew many more of the words than I did. She ordered artichoke dip, one of her favorites, and mini hamburgers, which she ate without the rolls. She had a glass of red wine. And she was rocking in her seat, singing along, and crazy to get up and dance.

Towards the end of the concert, I went to the bathroom, and as I was coming back, there was Maggie, threading between the tables to the stage. She had seen one woman at the front stand up, and that was all it took. She just couldn't contain herself any longer. She was beaming—I'll never forget that face. I stood and watched her and danced a little myself. She was turning around and scooping her arms, trying to get all the old fogies to stand up. And they did! Maggie told me later that the woman who had stood up first said, "This never happens at the Rams Head!" It certainly was the first time I'd seen everyone up and dancing. Maggie had made herself part of the band, electrifying the crowd.

Maggie stayed right up front, dancing and singing for the rest of the concert. Between songs, she was talking to the guys, giving the bass player a hard time about his LSU t-shirt and saying he should be a Trojan. She told them that the first album she ever bought was theirs, and the lead guitarist gave her his pick. She told John about how much her Dad had wanted to be there, and he gave her his harmonica to give to Bill. She was so excited and happy as she told Jim and me all about this on the ride back to Baltimore.

So, soon, Anita is going to crank up Blues Traveler's

"Optimistic Thought;" you'll find the words to the refrain printed in the order of service. In Maggie's memory, in her honor, as a promise to carry on with our lives despite this terrible pain we will always bear, I invite you all to get up and dance, to hug each other, and to sing your hearts out on the refrain!

November 13

Falling Asleep on the Beach

Jim and I took a long walk on the beach; it was a sweet, beautiful, sad time. We sat, side by side, against the dune, which blocked most of the wind. The sun was as high and as strong as it would get today. I pulled up my hood and lay back against the sand, which felt slightly warm. I closed my eyes, listening to the break of the waves, the pull of water against sand, a seagull crying. I felt the sun on my face.

The next thing I knew, I was awakening. I was so surprised at this gift: a short, deep, peaceful sleep on this dune in the sun, by the sea, next to the man I love.

November 14

I Love You. I Love You. I Love You.

The first person I saw after getting back to Baltimore was the youngest son of my oldest friend. Noel had made a special trip home from college to see me, because he would not be able to attend the memorial service. Maggie was close to his age; he also is an Ultimate Frisbee player and an actor; he too has a big personality. Noel and Maggie grew up together. I also am his godmother and his former teacher. It was natural that Maggie's death would touch him deeply, but this was something more.

Despite it being a busy time of the academic year, Noel flew to Baltimore for less than twenty-four hours to put his arms around me. And when he did so, he buried his face in my neck and said, "I love you. I love you. I love you." We sat together, drinking coffee, sharing a cinnamon muffin, talking about school and art, one's calling, romance, and family. It was a gift.

November 15

Friends and Family

My cousin Sandy and his wife Anne live in my grandparents' old house, the house my mother grew up in, the house where my wedding reception was held, the house my mother and her second husband lived in when Maggie was born. It is a special place for our family. Therefore, it meant the world to us when Sandy and Anne offered to host a dinner and to put up many of our friends who were coming from out of town for the memorial. The evening was casual and low-key, but warm and comforting. People arrived and left, and it was just wonderful to have that base from which to connect with everyone.

Midway through the evening, I received a call from one of Maggie's high school friends, telling me that a bunch of their group had gathered at the Towson Diner for dinner. My grad school friend Robbie said she would keep me company if I wanted to go over for a little while. One surreal detail from that drive was stopping at a light and the trunk of the car in front of us popped open and there was someone inside. I think now that I was less surprised than I should have been—everything was already so strange that a person riding in the trunk of a car seemed unremarkable.

A Memorial Service in Celebration of the Life of Margaret Oliver Feiss

11 July 1986   —   2 November 2008

*"Oh, I have slipped the surly bonds of earth
And danced the skies on laughter-silvered wings."
From "High Flight"
by Fl. Officer John Gillespie McGee*

1922-1941

Order of Service
November 16, 2008
Towson Unitarian Universalist Church
1710 Dulaney Valley Road
Lutherville, MD 21093

November 16

Memorial

My hair was a mess, it had gotten long and needed shaping. Karen, my hairdresser, bless her, came into her salon today, a Sunday, yes to do my hair, but also to help me along on the morning of my daughter's funeral. She knew Maggie; one of her stylists had cut Maggie's hair when she donated it for the first time to Locks of Love, saying that they would be able to get at least two, maybe three, wigs out of her mop of curls. And, of course, as my hairdresser, Karen knows me. She washed my hair herself and spent as much time massaging my scalp as washing. She did my hair this morning with love and affection, as much support in her touch as in her words.

I couldn't eat. I felt sick all morning. Bill, Stephen and I gathered at Bill's house to be together, to get dressed, and to await the limousine. We each had a part to play in the service, and I know we each seriously doubted our own ability to get through what loomed before us.

Though we arrived at the church a half hour early, the parking lot was overflowing and people already had begun to fill the chairs we had set up in the lobby outside the sanctuary. We learned later that the three hundred people whom we had estimated might attend Maggie's memorial service were indeed closer to five hundred. People had stood outside the church building just to be there, many others had come and gone. People gathered from everywhere, drawn by their wish to come together to celebrate what Maggie had meant to them and to stand with us in our terrible loss. The energy was electric.

Because we are Unitarian Universalists, we were able to plan a beautiful service which really did memorialize Maggie without any religious agenda. Stephen had collected songs which Maggie loved which were played for the Prelude and Postlude. My brother Bill assembled a beautiful slide show of photos, which Maggie's friends and family had sent him, which ran along with the music. Bill wrote and delivered the words for the chalice lighting, and family members and friends shared eight short eulogies. This was where Stephen and I came in. Though most of the eyes in the building were full of tears for most of the service, each of us was able to stand up and speak when our turn came. I know I was full of super-human strength throughout the entire service and indeed through the reception that followed.

Bill, Stephen, and I stood in one place for three and a half hours as people comforted us with hugs and kisses, hands held, kind words of love and memories of Maggie. I don't know how long people waited for these few moments to see and speak with us, but it was immensely moving to feel this outpouring of love.

Jim is a relatively new addition to my life compared with some of the people who were there, many of whom did not know him. Whenever I looked up to point him out to someone, he was somewhere within my line of sight, right there. The one time I couldn't find him, he was standing behind me.

Optimistic Thought

Jim was my back-up for the eulogy. Clare had insisted that if family and friends were to speak, we should have someone prepared to step in if needed. She said having back-up in place was good insurance that it would not be needed. As nervous as I had been before the service began, once it started, I was at peace. I did not need the beautiful pressed old, cotton hankies Robbie had brought me. I knew I would make it.

When I stood at the lectern and looked out at the church, brimming with people who shared my sorrow, I was carried. My head was high, my voice was strong. I read my eulogy well and even got a few laughs. Maggie came across in the story and then we moved into the dancing. Everyone was up! The music was uplifting and the lyrics, a perfect expression of what we all were feeling: a celebration of an amazing life.

People stood, hugged, smiled, swayed, and danced. I wove through the front of the church, receiving hugs and smiles, all through everyone else's tears. At one point I said out loud, "Why is everyone crying?" I really couldn't imagine. I traveled across one row and at the end was a group of my high school friends. "Oh, it's my girls," I said.

The song came to an end, people sat, I sat; it was perfect. I knew Maggie was happy and proud of me.

November 17

You Have Feelings?

I was reading condolence letters and felt so strange and detached—like what are these people talking about? I mentioned this to Stephen, saying, "I feel like this is all so surreal." And Steve said, "You have feelings?"

There is very much that too—the numbness, the incomprehensibility of it all.

November 18

The Scarf

In September, Maggie asked me to teach her to knit. We bought some yarn in Boston when we were there visiting Stephen, and she made a pink headband for Stephen's roommate, John. Once home, she made another headband, for Steve, and then dove into a gray wool scarf for her Dad. She was not wild about knitting and had told some friends that it really was not the hobby for her. But she was making progress on the scarf. I found her knitting project next to the bed she was in when she died. Several days ago, I began work on finishing the scarf for Bill. Simple knitting always comforts me, the mindlessness and repetitiveness of the task is very meditative. Having these needles which Maggie held, the yarn which she chose, and the project which she started in my hands makes me feel closer to her. There is so much left unfinished about Maggie's life, but this is one thing I can do.

Meg Tipper

November 19

Debrief With the Doctor.

I first heard the term SUDEP from our minister, Clare, as we were planning the memorial service. She had taken the time to do some internet research. I had assumed that Maggie's death was from a seizure, and this was what we identified as the cause of death in her obituary and in the announcement we created on Facebook. However, the fact is that the official cause of Maggie's death is SUDEP, Sudden Unexplained Death in Epilepsy Patients. It happens in 1 out of 3-4 thousand cases of people with epilepsy. By definition, there is no explanation for the death: no suffocation, no brain aneurysm, not even definite evidence of seizure activity; as Clare put it in her eulogy: "Epilepsy wore out Maggie's body in ways that the medical profession does not yet understand."

I wanted to meet with Maggie's neurologist, and Bill acquiesced. Eric Kossoff is a pediatric neurologist in practice at Johns Hopkins Hospital, an excellent doctor whom both Bill and I like and respect immensely and whom Maggie adored. We met for coffee after Eric got out of an evening meeting of the Abilities Network, for which he serves as a board member. Eric was very good with Bill, assuring him over and over that he had done everything right: there was nothing that he should have heard, that CPR would not have revived Maggie.

I asked Eric about his thinking about not telling caregivers about the risk of SUDEP. He said that they debate this issue in their practice and that some doctors make a different decision, but that he chooses not to mention SUDEP. If there were anything that knowledge could do to prevent SUDEP, he would not hesitate, but that is not the case. As it is, he spends much of his professional life helping parents to be less protective, to get the three year old out of his parents' bed. Eric also felt concerned about the anxiety levels that knowledge of SUDEP inevitably creates sometimes being worse than the disease itself.

I understand his reasoning, and it makes me consider that if we had known of this risk, would we then have felt obliged to tell Maggie as well as Maggie's friends, their parents, her teachers, her camp counselors, her housemates, and her traveling companions not only about the possibilities of seizures but also the possibility of death? How Maggie's life would have been altered, how her activities and options would have been limited, and still, the worst would have happened in the one place where parents think their child is safe: at home, in bed. As it is, she lived her life richly and fully and very independently, and it is her dear father who has been given this terrible burden of her death sometime that Sunday afternoon while he sat in his recliner in the living room, reading the paper and watching TV, thinking that his precious daughter was asleep upstairs.

Standing at the Edge

November 20

Ashes

Today, I picked up Maggie's ashes at the funeral home. Once home, I took the small, brown box and held it in my arms. It seemed surprisingly heavy, about the weight she was when she was born. I rocked it and cried. I opened the box and lifted out the can inside. I took the top off the can, slowly picked up the cushion of cotton, and there they were, the remains of my daughter's body: grey ash with very small chunks of white bone. There were snow flurries this afternoon.

November 21

Travel

Today my friend and former colleague, Linda Trapp, and I flew from BWI to Raleigh/Durham, rented a car, found the hotel, made it through a social event, and even survived a trip to the Emergency Room. But I ask myself, "Whatever possessed me to think I could do this?" I so wanted to keep my commitment to be with my former Gilman colleague, Shara, and Kristian for their wedding and to keep Linda company. I wanted to be there to see their smiles, to feel their joy. Still, I underestimated how much of an effort travel and socializing would be. I was happy to be there, but I also just wanted to be home, with Jim, with no decisions to make, nothing to figure out, no effort required.

November 22

How Many Children Do You Have?

At the rehearsal dinner, a handsome, kind young man struck up a conversation with me and asked the most innocent question, "How many children do you have?" I was completely undone. I looked into his eyes and burst into tears, but not lady-like tears that well up just inside the eyelids—no these were huge, really ugly sobs, and I couldn't stop. I had been told that such a moment would come when I would have to make the quick decision about whether to say two and go in or one and stay safe, but I wasn't prepared.

I finally blubbered out an explanation of why I was upset and then, of course, he fell all over himself to apologize. To his great credit, he did not take that as his cue to make a quick get-away for the appetizer table, but rather stayed and talked with me about Maggie, her life, and her death. I will never forget his kindness on the heels of his misfortune to have been the one to break me in with this question.

November 23

Chance Encounter

When Maggie and I were in Boston in September, we walked into Porter Square to buy some yarn and got caught in a downpour. We ducked into a bookstore/coffee shop to wait out the rain. Many others had done the same, and tables were scarce. We asked a pretty woman who was sitting alone if we could join her, and while I went to get napkins and pick up my coffee, Maggie started up a conversation with our table companion. We ended up enjoying each other's company and even exchanging email addresses.

As I was cleaning off piles on my desk and trying to get a bit organized, I found Kathleen's card. I realized that she is a counselor and that she might be a perfect resource for Stephen if he should need some help. I contacted her, and have just received her quick reply: of course she remembered our coffee together, was devastated to hear about Maggie's death, and was there for Stephen if he should want to talk. I feel like Maggie laid the groundwork for Stephen's support before she died, just in that chance encounter.

Meg Tipper

November 24

No One Knows the Troubles I've Seen

Jim was going to a hearing about a proposed local development project, which he anticipated many of the neighbors would oppose. When he asked if I would like to go, I warned him that I would be likely to listen to people complain about traffic congestion and the threat of losing the character of the neighborhood, and after awhile, I would have to stand up and scream, "Are your children dead?! If not, you have nothing to complain about!" He suggested that perhaps I should stay home.

November 25

Competence

I am used to being a very competent person. I can handle complex tasks, make good decisions, trust my judgment. I am organized and efficient, a good worker. And people are used to me being competent.

Today, I went to the grocery store and felt overwhelmed, I wandered the aisles, unable to find the feta cheese that was on sale or even to remember whether I had picked up the coffee filters or not. When I got home, Jim commented on something that I had bought that we hadn't actually needed, and I felt so angry. Did he not know how impossibly hard it had been for me to go shopping?

November 26

Fragile

Everything feels fragile to me. I have terrible fears about losing Jim, Stephen, my Mom, Bill. I have never been a clingy or over protective person, but I feel that now. I have tried to make a joke out of it, saying, "Don't die! You are not allowed to die right now!" But I am not joking. I don't think I could survive.

November 27

Phone Calls

My friends and family and the people in my twelve step recovery group have shown their support in so many ways; I have been overwhelmed with love. Sometimes I mean that literally. This balance can be particularly precarious with the phone. For awhile I tried to take all my calls, feeling that I needed to talk to people directly. But now I find my stamina for the phone is limited. I have to pace myself with how often I connect with someone else's grief. Sometimes I can't even summon the energy or presence for what likely will be a matter of fact conversation. Sometimes I want everyone to leave me alone. I hate feeling ungrateful; I hate feeling so fragile and incompetent that phone calls become a monumental deal.

November 28

No Shoulds

I am sure that this person meant no harm, but it was suggested to me that I should be trying to keep up with answering the letters of condolence as they come in so as not to get behind, lest the task become overwhelming. I was not gracious in my response. I think I said something like, "That's not possible right now." What I really wanted to say was, "Are you out of your freaking mind?!" I have to give myself permission to get through all of this in whatever way I can, recognizing the profound possibility that some people do not come out on the other side of losing a child. The old cliché that "God does not give us more than we can handle" is a load of crap.

November 29

May I Say a Prayer With You?

A fairly distant acquaintance (the parent of a former student) called me to touch base because she had been thinking about me. She had not heard about Maggie's death and when I told her, she was rocked. Responding slowly, she asked, "May I say a prayer with you?" I am not a religious person, but I do have a powerful, but quite private, spiritual life. I pray in my own way to a higher power of my own understanding. So, this question, is not one I often hear. And yet, when she asked, I said yes, without hesitation. It was lovely to receive her prayer for healing, to hear her earnest intercession to her Jesus for help for me and for all who loved Maggie.

Love, energy, healing, whatever name makes sense to whomever is humbled enough to know that such a loss is bigger than he or she can handle alone, these "prayers" have been uttered in all corners of the world in the last month for me and for our family. I feel them helping.

November 30

Making Decisions

Normally I am a decisive person. I know my mind. Maggie was terrible at making decisions. She once loved a leather jacket she saw in Venice but didn't buy it, traveled to Milan, then decided she wanted the coat, and returned to Venice to buy it. Even more extraordinary was the coincidence that she ran into some of her old friends from England on the train back to Venice! Now, I cannot decide about the most simple things. I really don't want to be asked what kind of herbal tea I want. I have no idea.

December 1

People Say Stupid Things

My friend left a breezy message on my voicemail, "Just checking in. Hope all is well." I'm sorry, but you're not allowed to say that to someone whose daughter has died a month ago. Fortunately she is a good enough friend that I could call and ask, "What was that about?" She said, "Well, sweetie, I meant under the circumstances." And I was able to say, "No, all is not well under the circumstances and never will be." I tell myself that people mean well and that they feel uncomfortable because, after all, what do you say? It makes me feel so ungrateful, but sometimes when people say, "How *are* you?" in that sincere way, I just want to get in their face and say, "How the hell do you think I am?!" On the other hand, if people don't acknowledge the loss, just go on with business as usual, I think, how can you ignore what has happened? There is no pleasing me.

If you had asked me if I'm angry about Maggie's death, I would have said no.

December 2

As the World Turns

In the first weeks, there was nothing in my consciousness except my dead daughter. It was all anyone talked about, all I thought about, and everyone around me was thinking about her too. There was great comfort in that. But now, I have to deal with the fact that the world is turning. Many things are going on besides the loss of Maggie. I have to begin to lead my life again.

At the grocery checkout, I started to reminisce with the clerk about my time in England with Maggie and how good we got at bagging for ourselves. She said, "I bet she lives there now." A beat, then I knew I wanted to tell her: "No, she died suddenly last month." The cashier came out from behind her counter and gave me a hug, "It hurts so much. My husband died suddenly six years ago, and it still hurts so much." We were both crying. It was an amazing moment. In the midst of returning to my life, I realize that I am just pretending, that I really just want and need to grieve. This loss consumes me. I want to hold Maggie close.

Meg Tipper

December 3

Walking Through Treacle

I went to DC to serve on a dissertation committee at George Washington University for a former colleague. I had read the dissertation, made careful notes, felt prepared. While it is the candidate who is most on the line, someone like me, a visiting member of the committee, is also being closely watched. Afterwards, the whole committee went to lunch and the conversation turned to our adult children and what they are doing. I mentioned Maggie, but did not go into what has happened. Part of me wanted everyone to know about her death, but of course the right thing was to keep the celebration focused on my colleague, the newly minted doctor. Still, when I returned home, I was irrationally annoyed with Jim, impatient, and quick to tears. It wasn't until then that I realized how exhausted I was, how much energy it had taken to function in the world for a day as a normal person. My friend in England whose husband had terrible depression said he called it, "walking through treacle."

December 4

No Patience for Your Pain

This is not an attractive side of me but right now, I don't want to hear about your problems. I find myself going into auto pilot when Gretchen goes on and on about her daughter's infection that ended her up in the hospital or Henry tells me that his girlfriend's best friend died. I say "I'm sorry, I am so sorry, how awful" but I am not feeling anything. Not only am I not feeling for them, I am feeling selfish, holding my loss to my chest and saying to myself, "This is my pain, this is all I can handle right now."

December 5

Done

I wake up this morning and I think, *Okay, I have been a really good grieving mother, I have planned a memorial service and read all the condolence letters and taken care of myself and been fairly gracious about all this and now I am done. I want to go back to being a Mom to my daughter now. I've passed the test.* But then, the test is just beginning, isn't it?

Meg Tipper

December 6

Food and Climbing

One of my first feelings on learning of Maggie's death was nausea. I never actually vomited, but I thought I might for about twenty-four hours. As my stomach got more and more empty, I felt better. Food made me feel sick, even the smell of it. I had a huge, hard knot in my stomach. Someone told me that that is the feeling of soul sickness. Finally, I ate a little soup; bread and butter tasted good after a day or two. Slowly I began to get my appetite back, but then food tasted terrible, and I couldn't eat. Then, when I began to eat, the food wasn't sitting well on my stomach. I lost a lot of weight. If I am honest, I would have to say that I liked the feeling of being empty. It matched my loss. It was something that I could feel that made sense to me.

Now, a month later, I am eating better, feeling better and stronger; I know a big part of that improvement has been getting back to climbing. I belong to Earth Treks, an indoor rock gym, and not only is it good for me physically to climb a few times a week, there is also some magic to focusing my mind on the problem of getting up the wall. There is tremendous comfort in thinking only about the next right move, while trusting that if I mess up and fall, I will be safely caught.

December 7

Snow Drops

My mother took a late afternoon walk and had a talk with Maggie: "I'm going to need a little sign that you are with me. When your Pop-Pop died, he would send the geese in the fall and I would know that he was close. Now, I'll just wait and you can let me know what your sign will be." Nothing. Well, Mom reasoned, Maggie never was one to do anything on demand. As Mom descended the hill, heading home, she saw a clump of snow drops, in bloom; snow drops, which usually bloom in April, were bobbing their perky heads happily in the November cold. Mom swears that they were not there on her way up the hill.

I watch myself with signs like this. Part of me clutches them, something here, concrete, to hold onto to keep myself from drowning in the emptiness of where Maggie is supposed to be, and part of me is skeptical, even cynical. She is dead.

Standing at the Edge

December 8

Holding the Feelings

Jim is a forester by training and I think he is very like a tree: deeply rooted, strong but flexible, stable. I have found more solace in him following Maggie's death than in anyone or anything else. It is partially his good nature, his sense of humor, his being a good listener, his thoughtfulness and generosity of spirit, but most of all, it is his ability to hold my feelings. Sometimes I can get very wound up and overwhelmed with sadness, gut-wrenching tears, desolation and despair, but he doesn't get scared. He doesn't have to run away or try to make me feel better. He stays and he holds me.

December 9

The Angels

Last Christmas I gave Maggie an angel ornament. She stands about four inches high and has her arms stretched high, her hands in fists, her chest full, and her head tilted up, proud and strong. She is the "Courage" angel. The tag reads, "Bringing a triumphant spirit, inspiration and courage." I found her among Maggie's things that she had with her at college. I remember at the time I bought it, debating about which theme to choose and deciding that Maggie's spirit most embodies courage. She was brave in ways that are so difficult for me: adventurous about new experiences, eager to meet and talk to new people, wild in her sense of fun, persevering but humble about the limitations caused by her disease. And now, she is finished with the struggle, and it is we, all of us who loved her and miss her so much, who need courage.

I bought a new angel ornament with Mom today. She is larger and her head tilts slightly down. Her hands are clasped, holding a star. She is the "Angel of Light." I have put both angels on my desk, between them, Courage and Light, Maggie and my higher power, we'll make it.

December 10

Rituals

I am leaving for England for the memorial service that Maggie's friends and former teachers are giving for her in York. One part of me is excited, full of anticipation to return to that land and people I love. Another part is full of trepidation. England is so much Maggie to me, especially York. We lived there and twice returned there together. We had so many rituals: going to see a movie at City Screen with Tracey, checking our email side by side at the Evil Eye Café, walking the city wall between the Bootham and Monk Bars, stopping at the chocolatier for dark chocolate covered ginger, eating fish and chips by the Ouse River and fending off the geese, strolling through the museum gardens, visiting at Bootham School. I am full of pain at the loss of my companion, the only person in my life with whom I shared that experience. I don't want to be sad all through this trip. My Mom and my Aunt Sally will be with me; my dear friends there will lift me up. I know there will be love and tears, and, I hope, healing.

December 11

Sisterhood

I passed the time on the flight to London by watching some movies, one of them the second "Sisterhood of the Traveling Pants." It wasn't very good, but it reminded me of going to see the first one with Maggie during our first Memorial Day weekend at Rehoboth Beach: shopping, movie, food marathon. I loved those long weekends; we had three during her college years to welcome her home and to help me survive the final weeks of school. The weekends were debauchedly girly, and we had the best fun, just the two of us. Perhaps because I had no sisters growing up, I loved these sorts of times with Maggie, when I didn't really have to be her Mom and could just be a girlfriend.

One time we loved to remember from Rehoboth was when we helped two blind girls find their way to Dolly's candy store on the boardwalk. We were having so much fun, and when we got inside, one of them took a deep breath of that sweet smell and said, "I am so happy, I feel like a kid in a candy shop. . . . Oh . . wait . . I AM a kid in a candy shop." We always loved to tell that story and laugh again over that classic line.

My Mom is lucky enough to have a sister, my Aunt Sally,

who lives in Paris. Sally will join us in York so that she will have a chance to mourn Maggie's death with us and also so that Mom will have some company while I spend time with some of my old friends.

December 12

Rainbows

Gill and Jonnie Usher welcomed Mom and me into their beautiful home in Norfolk with all the love of dear old friends. I had looked forward to being with them, knowing that not only would the company and the fire be warm, but I would also have my bracing walks along the salt marshes out to the sea.

The weather was "beastly" as only English weather can be, and I was getting very wet on my walk. *Maybe I'll just go back*, I thought, but then decided *no, I can get dry and warm when I get back, I want to keep going.* The sun behind me was getting squeezed between the horizon and the clouds, making everything luminous. The tidal flats and marshes glowed more and more golden as I walked. I began talking to Maggie, affirming that there is still beauty and happiness to be found and that I know she is with me. Suddenly, off to my right, where they would have been out of my sight if I had turned back earlier, were two rainbows, side by side, glowing against the black sky.

December 13

Silence

Today, the day of the memorial at Bootham School, broke cold and wet; the wind had howled all night. We left Norfolk before dawn, and it rained the whole drive to York. We gathered in the library of Bootham, chairs drawn into a wide circle, sunflowers and two candles on a table in the center, a slideshow of Maggie photos rolling at the foot of the room. Once again, the room was filled to the brim: friends from the Unitarian church, from the York recovery community, former neighbors, and, from Bootham, Maggie's teachers, coaches, dorm mother, nurse, librarian, school friends and some of their parents. More people crowded in and extra chairs were gathered at the last minute.

Before the tributes began, we spent ten minutes in silence as is the Quaker way. At first, the quiet time weighed heavily for me, but soon I settled into breathing, remembering, and being together. It was lovely.

Then, after the service was over and most people had left, the circle of silence was completed as the remaining few mourners gathered in the rain to scatter some of Maggie's ashes in the headmaster's garden. We each found our own place and moment to say good-bye.

Standing at the Edge

December 14

T-shirts

Before leaving for England, I was going through Maggie's clothes, wanting to find some things to bring with me. The answer was clear: T-shirts. The girl had hundreds of T-shirts, most from all her causes; they were perfect as a way to remember her. And so I packed a pile of T-shirts into my suitcase: Relay for Life, Ultimate Frisbee, American Cancer Society, Breast Cancer, Community Service Day, Gay Rights, Camp Can Man, and brought them to the memorial in York. And people not only grabbed them, they put them on! Her beloved house mother, Jenny Bailey, got the pink tie-dyed Hellions of Troy T-shirt and her dear Deputy Headmaster, Graham Ralph, donned the "Life is Good" T-shirt with the Frisbee catch. I was happy that everyone left feeling the spirit of Maggie very strongly and some left with something more tangible as well.

December 15

Sorrow and Sighing Shall Flee Away

Mom, Aunt Sally, and I went to the glorious York Minster for Evensong, something I have done many times but never tire of, despite my lack of any religious connection to the service. I love the boys' and men's choirs especially, and it was a treat to hear them this night. The Minster was chilly and damp, but I had dressed warmly and tried not to focus on my numb fingers and toes, just the warm light of the candles and the hearty tremble of that rich organ. The anthem was Samuel Sebastian Wesley's "The Wilderness," a gorgeous piece with long duets between one young boy soprano and a tenor. The refrain, which repeated like a chant was, "Sorrow and sighing shall flee away." And I believed it, feeling that the waves of grief will come, as they do, but also that they will pass quickly if I let them, surrendering to their enormity. The feeling was akin to the sound of the organ as it vibrates and fills the cavernous Minster and then settles again into silence.

December 16

Most Normal Day

Jennie and Tony Skeels took Mom and me for a walk around Coxwold. We actually had some sunshine, and it felt so great to be putting one foot in front of the other, climbing stiles, crossing fields, talking to the sheep, feeding the swans, enjoying the English countryside I love so much. Mom was a trooper. She walked two miles to the village and then warmed up in the pub until we returned for her. Of course, she made friends in the short time she was there. I told my dear friends that they had given me the most normal day I have had since Maggie died.

December 17

Wake Up

I have not had any dreams yet of Maggie alive. I find this amazing and perhaps proof of the power of her death on my mind. It is so strange that my mind will trick me into forgetting Maggie's death when awake but is so relentlessly true in sleep! Last night I dreamt that Maggie awoke. Her eyes flew open and she looked at me. Instantly, I had that dream awareness of itself—the thought—*this must be a dream*. And that was it. I long for the comfort of a dream of my vital daughter.

December 18

Rush Hour

I had to drive around the beltway at rush hour in the rain, a week before Christmas. It felt like more than the usual madness. It felt like a pace, a demand of attention, and a pressure that was almost too much to bear. I can't say that I was having a panic attack, but there were edges of that level of anxiety. I got into the right lane, drove with the flow of the traffic, and prayed. I asked Maggie to make everyone go home. That made me laugh and I felt better.

December 19

Girlfriends

Kathy, Helen, and Dee, with whom I have played bridge once a month for over twenty years, were with me last night. We had a fun hour and a half of cards and talk: Kathy's son's engagement, Helen's daughter's graduation, and Dee's daughter's upcoming wedding. I am truly happy for them and for their children, whom I have known all their lives and whom I love. But I reached a point when I needed to stop. I needed us to talk about Maggie, to remember her past because there will be no future, no new news of her. I pulled out a few of Maggie's clothes for my friends to choose from. To their great credit, they were completely attuned to my need for them to take a tangible reminder of Maggie with them, and they seemed to treasure those silly presents: pajama bottoms, a T-shirt, a flouncy skirt.

December 20

6:30am

It is still dark out; I've only been up for half an hour and have already cried three times. I try not to judge myself as either falling apart or having a bad day. I tell myself that this is not a day at a time process but rather a moment by moment uncovering of the most raw and tender feelings. Tears are as much a part of the grief that will be my companion for the rest of my life as is joy when dawn breaks on this, the darkest of days.

December 21

The Erection

I love that Jim saves tidbits from his day to make me laugh. Tonight at dinner he told me about two women who stopped to talk as he was working on the roof of the turret for our Victorian house that he has been constructing in parts in the driveway since August. One woman said, "We walk by often and have been watching your progress." The other chimed in, "It's so exciting. When are you going to get it up?" Jim stifled his laugh and told her that he hoped to get it up very soon.

December 22

The Celtic Knot Tattoo

On the way home from the funeral home, Bill, Stephen and I all rode in the back of the car Bill's brother Chris had hired for us. We were touching shoulders, sitting quietly at a light. Suddenly, Stephen said, "We should all go get tattoos." It was a great laugh, but also, instantly, we knew, a great idea, and it has taken hold with many of us who loved Maggie. There has been considerable talk about what the tattoo should be. Janet, my sister-in-law, came up with the idea of incorporating a peace sign because Maggie always signed her emails and often closed her voice mail messages with "Peace." The two of us decided that we would get our tattoos done now, during this visit with them in Florida at Christmas time.

Maggie had one tattoo, a Celtic Knot on the top of her right foot. As I thought about the Maggie tattoo I wanted to get, I kept the peace sign idea central, but also came to understand that this tattoo into my skin could serve as a source of comfort in a more tangible way. If I used a labyrinth, then I could trace the design with my finger, following the path of it to find some peace. I drew a traditional labyrinth design with a peace sign in the middle and took it to the tattoo shop with Janet. She too was trying to find her way into the right design, and we looked for awhile among the options at the shop. I found there a whole panel of Celtic knots, many of them much simpler than Maggie's, and I realized that these too can be followed as a kind of labyrinth. Jimbo, our tattooist, suggested that I could put a peace sign inside the knot, and we also decided to add some color, purple, my and Maggie's favorite.

I had always known that if I ever were to get a tattoo, I would have it done just inside my hip bone, where I can see it but most others can't. I knew it would hurt, but I didn't know it would hurt like hell, a burning, grabbing sensation, very intense. When it was close to being over, I cried. Relieved, but also very emotional about the commitment that I had just made, permanently marking myself in memory of my daughter. As my friend Claudia said, I had "burned her into my very flesh."

December 23

The Dolphin

My brother, Kendal, Jim and I were walking on the beach, a beautiful late afternoon sun starting to glow up the sky. I was talking about Maggie being my best traveling companion and feeling how much I would miss her company along my way. Clouds began to gather and Kendal said he felt a few drops of rain. I don't know what, but something made me turn around, and I was stunned by the beauty of the sky, the sun shooting all around in beams, the explosion of colors, and then, suddenly, there was a huge splash in what had been a very calm gulf, about twenty feet away. A single dolphin played there, cresting through the water, flipping around, so close! We all three stood and watched, transfixed, and then, just as suddenly, it was gone. It was a sweet visit and I felt comforted.

December 24

How Am I?

I posed this question to my dear brother. I am someone who generally has clarity about my state of mind. I would say I am self aware, I hope not too preoccupied with myself. Part of my daily prayer practice is doing inventory to see what I'm carrying around, but, since Maggie's death, I have been very unclear. People say, "I can't imagine how you are feeling," and I say, "I can't imagine how I am feeling." Feeling divorced from myself is foreign and disconcerting and, to my mind, potentially dangerous. And so I ask some people who know me well, who will tell me the truth, "How do I seem to you?"

December 25

Family Mourning

It was good to have a very different sort of Christmas—different configuration of people, different venue, no traditions that felt gapingly empty without Maggie. It was also very simple; no one had had much energy for planning or shopping, but we had a very meaningful Christmas nonetheless.

In the middle of the day, we drove to the beach for a walk in the sand and sun, such a luxury for Christmas Day. We were ambling along, chatting, when I realized that the family group just ahead of us, huddled tightly at the edge of the water, was spreading ashes. I turned and quieted everyone as we passed behind the mourners. The energy among us shifted immediately. Stephen came to my side and put his arm around me. I caught Kendal's eye. We walked on but were silent for a long time.

I was afraid that some of my gifts for Stephen focused too much on Maggie (a photo of the two of them, an old, soft nightshirt of hers, a box of Christmas ornaments that had special meaning to the two of them). He did get very emotional, "Mom, you're killing me!" But when I apologized later, sorry that my gifts had made him cry, he said, "That's not a bad thing." I felt like at least part of him appreciated this time to grieve together.

December 26

Sun

It has been beautiful in Florida for our entire visit. Kendal said the weather had never been better at Christmas time in all their years here. My spirits have been very good, despite the emotional weight of the holiday. I have to give some credit to being in the sun. Being warm, having the sun higher in the sky and the days longer, and taking long walks every day: these are key ingredients for a happier outlook for this girl. But now it is time to return home.

December 27

Time

I found a package of Christmas cards among Maggie's things. The picture is a copy of a painting by the artist Michelle Winters entitled "Chicago Water Tower." There is a clock in the foreground and written across the bottom of the painting in block letters is the message, "This is the time . . .Our only time . . . Live time. Now." It didn't surprise me that Maggie would have bought these cards. It was very much a part of who she was—this idea that life is precious, that life must be lived fully.

Shortly after Maggie died, I said to Jim that it seemed like she had made a special point to see people she loved and to have meaningful visits with them within the last weeks before she died, almost like she knew that her life was ending. Jim looked into my eyes and said, "but that was the way Maggie was all the time." And it was true. I'm trying to carry some of that passion into my own life: to respond openly, to appreciate, to savor, to embrace, and to accept it all as a rich gift.

December 28

Chocolate Chip Cookies

When I was in high school, I got a killer recipe for the world's best chocolate chip cookies. I copied the recipe onto an index card from my friend Sue's friend Mary. Maggie and I both loved to make these cookies. They were a particular favorite on snow days when school was closed. Over the years, the writing faded; the card got vanilla and egg spilled on it and became worn around the edges. Today, I wanted to make my cookies for a party. I pulled out the recipe, and there it was in Maggie's handwriting. I had completely forgotten that at some time, Maggie had recopied the recipe onto another index card. Now, not only are the recipe and the making of the cookies special, so is the card.

I never used to give this recipe away. Now I want all Maggie's friends to carry on the baking legacy. Here it is:

Mary's Awesome Chocolate Chip Cookies

Cream 1 c. Crisco until soft. Blend in 1 ½ c. sugar, 3 T. molasses, 2 t. vanilla, 2 eggs. Mix well. Sift in 2 c. white flour, 2 t. baking soda, 1 t. salt, 2 c. chocolate chips, 1 c. nuts (if desired). Bake at 350 for about 10 minutes on ungreased cookie sheets. Remove from oven before you think they're done if you want them to be chewy. Remove from sheets and cool on brown paper bags.

Mary's Choc. Chip cookies

Cream 1 cup of shortening (Crisco) until soft.
blend in 1½ cup sugar, 3 T. molasses + 2 t. vanilla + 2 eggs
mix well
stir in 2 c. unsifted white flour, 2 t. baking soda + 1 t. salt
2 c. choc chips + 1 c. nuts
Bake at 375° about 12 min. on ungreased cookie sheets
Cool on brown paper bags

(also - 1 c peanut butter + only about 1½ c. flour

Makes 4 doz.

December 29

Necklace

I have been slowly dealing with Maggie's clothes and other things. I have sorted out some special presents for her friends. I also wanted to save some things, maybe for a future daughter in law or granddaughter. So, I was going through Maggie's jewelry box, sorting, throwing some things away, keeping others, and getting others ready to give away. I polished some silver and then had some necklaces to untangle. I was doing fine. I was prepared to deal with her jewelry.

I lifted one particularly nasty tangle of necklaces up to the light and there, caught in the chain, were two strands of hair, Maggie's hair. I completely crumbled, held the hairs between my fingers and fell over, wracked with sobs. I was ready for jewelry, not at all prepared for strands of curly hair. Sometimes grief is predictable, sometimes preventable, and sometimes I am completely blind-sided.

December 30

I didn't think you would want to hear from me

Recently, one of my friends apologized for not being in touch. She said, "I didn't think you would want to hear from me." I found this feeling odd but after I thought about it, not surprising. After someone dies, we measure: how close am I? What level of intimacy and am I entitled to? How much contact from me is welcome and how much is too much?

I told my friend that I knew she was thinking about me and holding me close, that I knew she loved me. But I also told her that I love her and would welcome her phone call or email from time to time. For me, the contact is important.

December 31

Socks

I would have bought Maggie socks for Christmas. I hadn't ever thought about the fact that I loved to buy her socks until I received the most wonderful note from Jim's son Zeke's Russian girlfriend, Anya, about a month after Maggie died. I am going to keep her words because her English is so charming: "Meg, do you remember that small shop in Hakodate [Japan]? Did Maggie like those funny socks you found for her there? They were cool, don't know why I haven't got a pair. Do you know why I remember it well? My mom is always buying me the socks. Every time I thought - oh... socks.. again.... and one day I understood that no one else was giving me the socks. Only she does, because she cares about these 'simple' things like giving the socks to her child. I don't know I felt like I should tell you the story. No matter how silly that was."

January 1

The First

All along the way, there has been the slam of first times without Maggie. It seems so silly, but one of the hardest has been going into Starbucks. It was something we loved to do—get coffee together—and we did it often. Not only have I not felt ready to go in, sometimes just seeing a Starbucks will either upset me or piss me off. I have been feeling like—*do they really have to be on every damn corner!*

Now, I'm better, but I still don't hang out there.

January 2

Note

Maggie's friend Alex wrote that she and her boyfriend, Nate, who was a roommate of Maggie's, "have an old note that Maggie left one morning stuck on our fridge. It says, 'Please don't leave w/o me...I don't have an alarm that I know how to use. Sincerely, Boss.'"

January 3

Haunted

When I looked at Maggie's body in the bed at Bill's house, I immediately turned away from her distorted face, but my eyes came to rest for a moment on her hand, gnarled into a claw. The image haunts me.

January 4

Die Hard

As I went through Maggie's DVDs and found the entire *Die Hard* series, I remembered having made a promise to her, which I had yet to keep. We were in Hollywood and Maggie went wild when she saw Bruce Willis's hand and shoe prints with "Yipee kiyay" written above them. I asked what it meant, and she gave me the withering look that only a daughter can give her mother and said, "I can't believe you haven't seen the *Die Hard* series. You have to promise that you will watch them with me. We'll have a marathon!" I promised, and we talked about it, but never got around to it.

So, this first weekend in the new year, when almost everyone else in Baltimore was watching the Ravens beat the Miami Dolphins, as many of Maggie's friends and family whom I could drag out gathered at Jim's house and watched *Die Hard* movies non-stop. The kids reminisced about the times they had watched with Maggie while John McClane got bloody—apparently she just couldn't get enough of the action, the chase, and the triumph of one man over all those bad guys.

January 5

Hi Momma

Jim's son Zeke is visiting from Moscow for the Christmas holiday, and we took him and his girlfriend, Anya, to DC for some sightseeing. It was sweet being with the kids, but Zeke was sick with a flu that was moving into his chest and making him feel miserable. Of course, all my mothering came out, though I tried to keep my advice and tending in check. In the afternoon, Zeke's mother, Anne, called to check up on him. I half listened as he talked, beginning the conversation with, "Hi Momma." His voice went up a little, that reaching out sound of the child wanting to be comforted. It was just what Maggie would have said. I turned my head and looked out the car window, not wanting anyone to see my tears.

January 6

Mourning the Future

I had a visit with one of my oldest friends. It was very easy to cry with her, the two of us crying together. A few years ago, her son told her that he is gay. I asked her if she had gone through a period of mourning the future she had imagined for her son. She said that all she really worried about was her son's safety. I shared that I have just begun to mourn the future, to think about all that I will miss that was yet to come: Maggie's accomplishments as an adult, her loves, her children, and yes, even her troubles. I had been busy making myself feel better by rationalizing that she was saved from the compromised life that having epilepsy forced on her. That perhaps she never would have found someone willing to love and care for someone with a serious seizure disorder, that her body might not have allowed her to be the mother she so much wanted to be. But the fact is that I did imagine her doing everything she wanted to do: traveling the world, fixing Baltimore, falling in love, getting married, having children, taking care of me in my old age. Now I have to begin to let myself suffer not only the real losses of the Maggie who was already in my life so vibrantly, but also the future I imagined we would have together.

January 7

Dentist

My six month dental appointment marked the last event on my calendar which I'd booked for Maggie. We would have been together, going to get our teeth cleaned and then having lunch and probably going shopping or seeing a movie or getting a pedicure. Instead, I went alone, received very loving condolences from the dentist and her staff, and cried. There I was, biting down on the stupid x-ray thing in my mouth and wondering if the machine would pick up the tears on my cheeks.

January 8

Delete Beneficiary

I realized that Maggie was one of two beneficiaries on my retirement plan. I have mixed feelings about this sort of business around her death. On the one hand, I resist it and feel it to be petty and bureaucratic and an impersonal sort of erasing of Maggie's presence. On the other, I like to take care of things that can be taken care of, to accomplish something that needs to be done. I went to the website, logged on, and then read through. The change couldn't have been simpler; it was a matter of clicking an icon. I know there must be reasons other than death to make such a change, but I can't imagine that many of them are positive. Maybe there is comfort to some in the anonymity of it, no explanation required, but for me, "delete beneficiary" was a difficult mouse click.

January 9

Grief Labor

Jim was driving us home after a visit with Mom. I was thinking about Maggie when she was little, remembering how she loved to dress up and her sense of style, even as a child. As I pictured her in some of the clothes she loved, the tears started to build, and I had a quick thought, "Oh God, here it comes." And it was a hard cry, not the quiet, sighing, shoulder shaking cry I sometimes have, this was one of the really sobbing, snotty cries. It rose to a peak and then slowly subsided. Jim is very good at these times, not scared, just present for me and my pain.

Later I reflected that these waves of grief are like labor. Between the contractions, I am lulled into thinking that I am okay, that I can handle what is happening to me. But then the contraction begins and I have that grab of desperation, of fear of the pain, and the pain builds, and I am consumed and wracked, and I feel like I can't stand it for another second, but I do. I am very conscious of this strange circle, the labor to bring my child into the world and the labor to see her out.

Meg Tipper

January 10

Thoughts that Make Me Feel Guilty

This is different than feeling guilty about Maggie's death. I have read about that being a common reaction. I know that Bill suffers terribly from his guilt that there was something he could or should have done to prevent her death—such a terrible burden. Thankfully, I am not carrying much of that sort of shame, but I am ashamed of some of my thoughts; here they are.

I am relieved not to suffer watching Maggie have seizures or to fear that she will be hurt during a seizure. I am relieved not to have the sadness that came with the compromises she was having to make in the way she wanted to lead her life. These thoughts don't seem so bad, but I even have thoughts about feeling relieved that I won't be inconvenienced by Maggie's dependence on me. As the economy takes a dive and I watch my retirement money disappear, I feel comforted that I will not have big medical bills to pay for Maggie or that I won't have to support her. I even have thoughts that it will be better for Stephen to inherit both his parents' financial resources without having to split them with his sister. Admitting these thoughts feels terrible; how can I be so petty, selfish, unfeeling, unfair, and callous? I am

Maggie's mother and she is gone, and there is this part of me that is seeing some good in her death, not in the spiritual sense, but in this really cold, practical, financial sense.

January 11

Loose Change

I have decided that whenever I see loose change, I am going to pick it up, even if it's just a penny. Everything I find will go into a little bank I've made for the Maggie Feiss Fund. I see it as a gift from Maggie, a way that she can contribute. Since I've come to that decision, I see change everywhere! There also has been so much change among Maggie's things. I never realized how my daughter left her own change everywhere: pockets, suitcases, pocketbooks, gym bag, make-up case. So, it was a hallmark even before she died and now, a perfect way to send her gifts my way! I see a coin and I say, "Thanks Mags," as I pick it up.

January 12

Letting Go

I rarely have trouble sleeping, but when I do lie awake in the darkest and coldest hours, it takes awhile for me to realize that I am holding on, keeping my body tight against the pain of grief. I don't know what this resistance to the mourning is about, whether it is instinct to avoid pain or some habit of my upbringing or personality. Nonetheless, it never fails that when I relax and let go, give myself to the great powers that are carrying me, and soften to the loss, then I am comforted and I can fall asleep.

This has been the greatest lesson I have had to learn and relearn in my long recovery through the twelve steps: that I can let go and trust a power greater than myself.

January 13

Voice of my Lowest Moment

Jim and I have been together for two and a half years and have committed to one another as much as two marriage adverse people can. We had been living together for awhile, but I had dragged my feet about actually moving, mainly because of Maggie. My apartment was our space; she had her room and most of her things were there; she used it as her permanent address; it was the closest thing she had to a home. After Maggie died, my apartment seemed suddenly empty and senseless. I knew it finally was time to move and told my dear landlords, Marty and Leo, that I would be out after the holidays.

As I made decisions about what I would take to Jim's, I felt that nothing had value. My furniture, my clothes, my books were all part of another life and now I didn't care about them. On the one hand, it was a sort of Zen feeling, a transcendence of the material things that clutch at us, on the other hand, it looked like depression.

I shared these feelings with Jim and with some people in recovery whose counsel I value, and they all said: "Do not make any decisions you will regret later. Do not listen to the voice of your lowest moment." We rented a storage unit and

I packed up many things. Later I may open the boxes and think, *Why the hell did I keep that?* but I may also think, *Oh, I'm so glad I didn't throw that away.* That said, we also will have one enormous yard sale in the spring; I had a lot of stuff I knew not to save.

January 14

Namesake

Maggie was my namesake and not only mine. There is a long line of women named Margaret Oliver, going back to the original, the daughter of Robert Oliver, a prominent merchant from Baltimore. It is an extraordinary legacy, perhaps unique, as so often this handing down of a name is reserved solely for the men of a family. Growing up, I thought I would name my own daughter anything but Margaret, such an old fashioned name, and surely no child should have to have a middle name like Oliver! But, as I grew older, the connections to my mother and grandmother carried more and more meaning and by the time Maggie was born, there was no doubt that I would seize the chance to name my daughter after the two women I loved and admired most. Now the chain has been broken. Rather than my daughter carrying my name into the future, I will carry hers. Margaret Oliver Feiss will not have a daughter to give our name to. Perhaps someone else in the family will name a daughter after Maggie, but something will have been lost.

Meg Tipper

January 15

Now You Can't See Me

Very soon after Maggie's death, I asked Jim to move all of her things from her room into my closet. She had shipped home big boxes from California after her graduation, and they were overflowing with things she had pulled out, looking for whatever she needed. Her clothes and shoes were all over her room. It wasn't so much that she was a slob, just that she had so many better things to do than organize her stuff. Anyway, while I was at a meeting, Jim tackled her room and was finishing up when I returned. I glanced at the bed and saw that all the stuffed animals were gone, and I said, "Oh, you put Scruffy away." That was her old beat-up, beloved, stuffed dog. Jim gestured towards the bookshelf and that was when I noticed that he was crying. There, he had created a little shrine: Scruffy, a picture of Maggie, her name tag on a lanyard, and, of course a Jim pun, a camouflage T-shirt that says, "Now You Can't See Me."

I left that shrine right there, except for Scruffy, whom Stephen took to Boston. It was one of the last things I packed up, and I brought it to my new home.

January 16

You've Reached Maggie

My aunt Doan-Doan, Maggie's godmother, told me that she has been calling Maggie's cell phone to hear her voice. I hadn't thought to do that, but was pleased that Bill had not cancelled the account and now I have called several times. The message is so typical of Maggie and today, when I called, I really listened, not just to her beautiful voice, but to the content: "Hi. You've reached Maggie . . . well, not really, but . . . you know what to do." What a message! There are so many times, every day, in which I feel this to be true: that in my prayers, in my thoughts, in my dreams, I reach Maggie, in some way, and she reassures me that I know what to do.

January 17

Sanctuary

After the movers cleared out my apartment and were packing the truck, I spent about ten minutes wandering quietly through the empty rooms. I came here exactly five years ago with my marriage broken. I had no idea how to be a single person or how to make a home for my cat Leah and me. Maggie was so angry, mostly at the situation, but it came out towards me a lot, and she stayed mostly at our house with Bill. It was important to me that she feel like she had a home with me as well and that we hold something like a family together as she finished her senior year of high school.

It is a wonderful, third-floor apartment with so much personality. The ceiling slopes down under the eaves and there are lots of closets. Maggie and I painted her room together, chose a new duvet cover, bought towels, and hung pictures. We both loved taking long, luxurious baths in the big, claw-foot bathtub. We both loved looking out at the tree-tops and pretending that we were living in a tree-house. We loved the radiator heat, the sound of rain on the roof, the cries of the geese. We loved to walk around Circle Road or over to Lake Roland. Her friends would come visit, climb the steep stairs, and we'd watch movies, make cookies, listen to music, laugh. To have our family split up was not what either of us wanted, but, over time, we were able to make a happy home.

January 18

My Back

Yesterday, I was on my feet from 7:45 until 2:15: up and down stairs, carrying boxes, making decisions. I was happy to be moving in with Jim and I know he was happy too. Still, around 1:30, my back started seizing up. It was cold outside and it felt like the muscles along my spine were all twisted up. I came home, took Ibuprofen, lay on moist heat, slept. By this morning, I felt better, but I realized that all day, I hadn't cried. It was the first day without tears. I came close when Jim gave me a little welcome card that he made, but I think I was too steeled, just needing all my focus and strength to make it through the day, but I paid a price in physical pain.

January 19

Bereaved Parents

So often now people tell me about children who have died. I remember when I was pregnant and all of a sudden, there were pregnant women everywhere. On a much less esoteric note, but perhaps one that men can relate to, when I am in the market for a new car, I notice cars. Well, obviously cars are everywhere, but I notice the *make* of cars. Likewise, when I have learned a new word, then I see it in use. I don't know if there is a name for this phenomenon. Yesterday someone I met at a meeting told me of his son's murder, the result of a tragic fight during post-college graduation revelry. We shared that look into one another's eyes, another parent's pain. He told me about the support group Bereaved Parents, which has been some comfort to him; I've invited Bill to go with me.

January 20

Inauguration Day

It was a huge day for our country, the first African-American elected to the office of president, swearing the oath of office before millions of people who had gathered in DC in the freezing cold to bear witness, along with billions of others around the world. I watched the television for hours. Even the inane commentary of the reporters could not diminish my excitement or the strength of my emotions. I felt Maggie all through the event. Barak Obama was elected president two days after her death; Bill put aside his own Republican loyalties and cast her vote for her. She was reveling in the energy, the hope, the unity, and the love.

January 21

Bad News Free Zone

My brother Charlie called me and left a message on my voice mail: "I'm afraid I have some bad news." I went cold when I heard that. Then he explained that Stephen's girlfriend had fallen while skiing and that they were at the emergency room, that probably the injury was bruised ribs, painful but not dangerous. When I told Bill about that message, he said, "I think we need to declare ourselves a bad news free zone." I wish that were possible. I have to be careful not to think that suffering my child's death makes me immune to anything bad happening to me or the people I love. Not that I am the sort of person to worry about or prepare for the worst, but I just don't want to work myself into a kind of good karma entitlement mind-set.

January 22

Circle of Pain

Bill and I attended a meeting of Bereaved Parents. Because there were new people present, everyone told the story of his or her child's death; every death was sudden. There were twelve people there, eleven parents and one best friend. Very much present were the eight dead children: two who took their own lives; one who was murdered; one who was struck by a truck while crossing the street; three, including Maggie, died from medical complications; and one died from SIDS. We were of diverse races, ages, personalities, but we were united by a common tragedy. As Bill said to me, "In this group, grieving a dead child is normal."

After about an hour, I could not wait for the meeting to be over; I felt like I was suffocating on the pain, my own and others'. And yet, I know I will go again. I don't understand that impulse: a combination of attraction and revulsion, but this whole experience of grieving Maggie's death is characterized by extremes and contradictions, so I just accept it and go with it.

Later, one of my friends in recovery suggested that perhaps the draw is in being able to do something with Bill to mourn together. That rings true to me.

Meg Tipper

January 23

Fireflies

I had not seen Maggie's oldest friend Linette in maybe fourteen years, but it was a joy to reconnect with her today and to remember the younger Maggie. They became close friends when they were in the same two year old daycare program. They went to elementary school together, played on the same soccer team, and remained friends until they finally drifted apart in middle school. Facebook was the vehicle for their reunion this fall, just about six weeks before Maggie died. Linette told me that when she heard of Maggie's death, her first thought was, *No, no, that can't be, we have plans to get together again*. I think there is particular poignancy in having regained a treasured friendship, only to lose it again so quickly.

Linette told me her favorite memory of Maggie was of a very warm summer night when they were up late and playing in our backyard. They were both enchanted with the fireflies glittering in the trees; they felt like fairy princesses. I think I remember that night and sharing in their delight. I told Linette that the fireflies are always at their peak around Maggie's birthday, fireflies and wild raspberries, both of which Maggie loved, both of which will always remind me of her.

January 24

Heaven

Heaven is not part of my vocabulary, but I understand that it has meaning for Christians, and I try not to resist the comfort that people are trying to give me who use that term. Someone told me that she had found solace after her best friend died, suddenly and very young, in thinking that she was waiting for her in heaven. I was not very gracious in that moment; I said something like, "But first she wants you to really live your life."

This assertion was about my need to root myself in life, despite the pain, despite the enormous hole I feel and the way I miss Maggie so much it takes my breath away. I have to feel that I owe it to her not to turn my back on the gift of my life, because if I really thought about Maggie wanting me to be with her in heaven, it would be too easy to go.

January 25

Dinner Table

Jim and I have stopped at my old friends, Anne Marie and Gregor's house, for the night on our way to New Hampshire for a week of skiing. Baltimore was cold but brown, and Gloucester is colder and white. Last night, we walked to Anne Marie's sister, Mary Tess's house for her Saturday night dinner, very bundled up, but delighting in the crisp air and crunchy snow. There was no moon, but the snow enabled us to see perfectly well in the woods without a flashlight. The stars were close and brilliant in the bare branches.

The last time I had dinner at Mary Tess's was in September with Stephen and Maggie, and Maggie's friends, Gardy and Scout. Last night, I deliberately sat at a different place at the table, but Maggie's absence was palpable for all of us who were there in September.

Perhaps there is some blessing in our family having been already both dispersed and broken; there was no nightly dinner table from which Maggie was suddenly missing. Bill suffered that loss to a greater degree than anyone else, because Maggie was living with him when she died. But it was not in the same way as it would have been for our family to face an empty chair in those days when it was the four of us having dinner together every night.

All through dinner, Jim was very attentive. He made a point of sitting next to me; even though he wasn't there in September, he realized I needed that extra support.

January 26

How Long?

I asked Annie whether all this time after Galen's death she still feels like part of her is missing, and she said no, she feels that she has healed. She talked about how some people hold onto the pain but that she couldn't live that way. I said for me, right now, the loss is so physical: a heaviness in my chest, weariness in my body, cloudiness in my mind. She said this will pass, it will change, and maybe after some years, I will just feel Maggie with me in a way that is enough.

January 27

Ultimate

I finally dreamt of Maggie alive. There was no great significance to the dream; she was playing with the Hellions of Troy, her women's Ultimate Frisbee team. It was a highlight of her college years, one of her favorite things, and something I never saw her do, much to my chagrin. In

the dream, she had played hard, but the Hellions had lost, and she was tired and dirty and a little peeved at me. I was amused because she used to do that when she was little: take it out on Bill and me when her team lost.

When I woke up and realized that Maggie had been alive in my dream, at first I was sorry that the dream hadn't been about some really special connection between us or at least that we had shared a positive feeling, but now that I've written about it, I am happy for the normality of it. It was a gift of something I had always wished to do with her and it probably was much like it would have been.

January 28

Books

At first I couldn't read at all. I was in the middle of a long and quite difficult book which I was really enjoying, but I haven't touched it since. The first reading I did was of the beautiful poems in Catherine Barnett's collection about the deaths of her nieces, *Into Perfect Spheres Such Holes are Pierced*.

Perhaps coincidentally (though I am suspicious of what appears to be coincidence now), both Kendal and Janet had read and enjoyed *Good Grief* by Lolly Winston while they were away on their long cruise in September. When I finally felt ready to tackle a novel, that was perfect, like a self-help book on grieving in novel form, and very funny. Everything Sophie Stanton does in the wake of her husband's death is a funny extreme of what I was feeling and doing, but she is so much worse, it made me feel better. Okay, so I couldn't manage to get the groceries, but I wasn't at the store in my pajamas.

Then I read Ian McEwan's *Enduring Love*, which also helped in a strange way because it began with a sudden death, from which so much difficulty unfolded. It made me think about how obsession works and to realize that aspects of grief are obsessive, that in a way my mind has been taken hostage by this loss.

When I was in Florida, I began *A Widow for One Year* by John Irving, thinking that I was tackling another widow book, safe. Well, the main character, Ruth, does become a widow, but way before that, and the shoals that underlie her life and the book, are the sudden deaths of her two brothers before her conception, and her mother's inability to allow herself to love her, the substitute child. The mother, Marion, haunted me, as Irving intends her to, but I couldn't let Marion go because I feared her. She was the mother who grieved forever, who not only lost her sons, but lost herself, her life, and her ability to love. A mother's grief is this ferocious force to which it would be so easy to succumb. Surviving is a monumental accomplishment, overcoming is heroic.

And now I am reading the book which has moved me to write of all the others. I had heard about Joan Didion's *The Year of Magical Thinking* when it came out in 2005 and stored it away as something I might read if the time were right. Then my friend Diane reminded me of it, and I have begun what promises to be a difficult but inspiring journey. I have to confess, I am already jealous: Didion is brilliant and an accomplished writer, and she undertook to do what I am doing, to record the aftermath of a sudden death and is doing it so much better than I! I'm not going to stop writing though; it is saving me.

January 29

Snow

Jim and I have come to New Hampshire for some skiing, an escape. As we drove away, we wondered why we were leaving the raw January of Baltimore for New England, but I looked forward to the bite of dead-winter cold here. For our first days of skiing, the sun was low but bright, so glorious as it caught the snow on the branches of the evergreens. And then today it snowed, and we stayed in, snug and warm, with the two fireplaces going, the world reduced to gray, and everything so quiet. With the edges of the world softened, I hoped that my feelings might be equally muted, but no. I remembered snowstorms when the kids were little and thought about what Maggie and I would do if she were with us. I carried her through the day, perhaps a little more peacefully, but nonetheless there.

January 30

A Good Day

Jim and I skied on fresh powder all day, challenging for us, weight, balance, turn. There were very few people on the mountain, no lift lines. We snuggled as we rode the lifts, always just the two of us. We enjoyed the same trails, were ready for a break at the same time, shared our fries at lunch, were both ready to call it a day. How lucky we were to have a day like this: to be retired, to have the means to ski, to have bodies still healthy enough to exercise, and to enjoy each other's company so much. On the way home from the mountain, I took Jim's hand and said, "I had a good day, baby." "I did too, baby." It was not lost on either of us that a good day is something to cherish.

When Bill and I were at the Bereaved Parents' meeting, one father said that he and his wife still had good times. She interrupted him, saying, "No, not good times, maybe okay times, there are no good times any more." He looked a bit sheepish. That made me mad.

I want it to be okay to have good times after my child has died. I don't want to tell myself that living a full and good life is somehow disloyal; I don't want to feel like being happy means I've failed to measure up as a grieving parent.

Meg Tipper

January 31

Doubt

I have been reading Didion's keen observations about the workings of her mind. By necessity, she becomes skeptical as she realizes how her mind tricks her. I am afraid that the "magical thinking" of the title will turn out to be more than just the irrational belief that her husband John will return, that Joan must keep his shoes so that he will be shod, stay at home so that he will know where to find her. I am afraid it also will be the turns of mind that provide another kind of comfort, the "signs" we receive from our beloved that he or she is still with us. I don't want Didion to enflame the doubt my rational mind already has about the legitimacy of these connections I feel to Maggie. I need to believe in them.

February 1

Snuggle

Stephen came up to New Hampshire to ski with us for the weekend. It was so good to be with him; I could feast my eyes on my son, and we had a great time skiing together. I had brought him a few more of Maggie's things: the drum she brought back from Ghana and the quilt that she and I made from African fabric, but we hadn't really cleared any space for Maggie time. This morning we were to part: Stephen to return to Boston, Jim and I to head to Burlington to see my brother and his family. Before I got up, I said my prayers and asked if there were anything I should do for Stephen. Immediately, I knew.

I crawled into his bed and snuggled with him, just like we used to do when he was little. For a long time, we just woke up slowly together, then I began telling him about the night of Maggie's death, when we knew and he didn't. Then I asked him about that next morning when we called with the news, what he had done, how it had been for him before he got to Baltimore. He opened up, speaking slowly, crying. I felt so grateful that he could do that.

February 2

Three Months

I had trouble sleeping last night, awoke and then couldn't get comfortable, was too hot, felt the edges of Maggie, in my dreams or just in my soul, had a nagging headache. One of the thoughts was of the three month mark, one quarter of a year, which felt significant. Maybe if I am still standing after three months, I will make it.

On the other hand, I suspect time has no meaning that I understand. During the two weeks after Maggie's death, I thought I would remember every detail. My senses were so heightened, it seemed impossible that I would not carry every second of such an indelible experience for the rest of my life. However, now, the memories are fuzzy. I suppose it is time that has dulled them, but perhaps it is also some self preservation akin to what kicks in to allow women to go through labor again.

I went to a twelve step meeting tonight in Burlington and watched as a newcomer picked up a token to mark three months of recovery. I shook his hand and told him that we had both been through great changes in the last three months and I wished him well. He seemed touched.

February 3

Another Tattoo

Jim and I have not seen my youngest brother, Charlie, and his family since Maggie died. As I was putting lotion on my tattoo, it occurred to me that I had not shown it to my nephew Jack. I knew he would be interested, because he has been thinking about his own Maggie tattoo.

I found Jack in his room, on the computer, as usual. I have not really connected with Jack in years, but we had a great talk about tattoos, the significance of the memorial tattoo, and the hazards of getting one at any age, but especially at fifteen. We discussed where he might put his tattoo and some different designs he is considering; he said he wanted something unusual, but using the peace sign, and something which would remind him of Maggie. I said that the other symbol she really loved was the yin yang. Online, he found a yin yang made out of peace signs, which he really liked. "I would like to get this done right now, with you, while you're here," he said. I was very touched. We compromised on a visit to check out the tattoo parlor and to talk to them about everything.

It was such an amazing adventure to share: walking into town, Jack talking to the receptionist at the tattoo parlor, hearing the restrictions and getting his head around them. We looked at the portfolios of the different artists who work there and chose our favorite. On the bus back home, Jack talked about his girlfriend, what his friends and he are doing with respect to alcohol and drugs, how he is concerned about some of his girl friends who are cutting. Once again, there was good flowing from Maggie's death, stripping through the awkwardness of a fifteen year old boy opening up to his fifty-six year old aunt.

February 4

Old

I glimpsed myself in the mirror and was shocked at the woman I saw. *Old* is not exactly the right word, there is a new frailty to my face, a vulnerability. In some ways, it is the look of a younger woman, one less self assured than she was in October; in other ways, my face is now marked with the ravages of loss that only age can carve.

February 5

Home

I like being at home. There is some small comfort in the routine and the familiar. In Joan Didion's book, *The Year of Magical Thinking*, she wants to be home because she believes that when her husband John returns, it will be to their home. I have had no such illusion. While my mind plays tricks, none is so effective as to make me think, even for a moment, that Maggie will return to us. It is just that home feels like a safer place in a life that is full of dangerous turns of emotion and little energy for navigating them.

February 6

Stephen's Girlfriend

Stephen has broken up with his girlfriend, which is a good thing over the long term but hard right now. I know it especially hurts to pull out of that relationship because going through the emotional intensity after Maggie died definitely catapulted them into more intimacy and dependence. Another thing that Stephen and I have talked about that makes the break up hard is that his girlfriend knew Maggie. Now, anyone he gets involved with after this, whomever he falls deeply in love with and wants to marry will never have met his sister. He will make Maggie as real as he can, but something true and dear will never be recaptured.

February 7

Crying

I have cried almost every day for three months. Now not as often as early on, but still the tears come quickly and easily. I rarely fight them; they are some relief. However, sometimes my eyes get tired and dry; it's weird that eyes can get dry from crying. Sometimes I need to close my eyes to rest them, sometimes just to shut the world out.

February 8

Mornings

I am ambivalent about the morning. On the one hand, I love my slow coming into the world, the closeness I feel to the spiritual realm, the easy break of light in the room, the warmth of our cozy nest in the bed and the cold of the air. On the other hand, I hate the slam of the realization of Maggie's death which always hits me as I gain consciousness, the heaviness of facing another day with this loss, the difficulty of getting out of bed in the cold.

February 9

Is There Anything Else I Can Do?

In going through Maggie's things, I remembered that she had an online gallery with Kodak. I found contact sheets from orders with great photos that I don't have, and I wanted them. So, I embarked on what I did not realize would be a four hour mission. I could not get access online; I followed the endless phone tree to a live person who told me I would need to speak to a supervisor tomorrow. I called again today, wound through the menu, climbed the chain of command until I finally reached someone who could help me. The transaction was efficient; I had held it together all this time. Everyone had been matter-of fact, and so had I. At the end of the call, the agent asked, "Is there anything else I can do?" and the thought jumped into my mind: *Bring her back, make this not be happening.* The tears rushed up and I could barely say, "Just tell me you are sorry that I lost my beautiful daughter." She paused, "I'm sorry," her voice broke, "I am so sorry."

February 10

Miss Optimistic

This morning I finally had a call from one of my dearest friends. I had left him several messages and had not heard back and when that happens, it's usually because he is depressed. So, when we finally spoke, I got busy trying to convince him that there is plenty to live for. I looked on the bright side, that all his challenges at work might be the beginning of a new start. I also minimized how incredibly awful it is for me to be living one day after another without Maggie. But no matter what I said, neither of us was feeling better. So, finally, when I couldn't make any of our sadness go away by being Miss Optimistic, the tears came, and then I couldn't stop crying. It rocked me for the whole day, not just the overflow of emotion, but also the sense that I had been so off in what either of us had needed as true friends. I also felt guilty that I had denied Maggie. I can gloss over the pain with an acquaintance, but not with a dear old friend who loved her too. I have to be alert to Miss Optimistic; she tries to steal the truth.

February 11

Ted's Room

It was so exciting to see Jim's turret project that he has worked on for half a year come together (literally). Finally, in an hour and a half this morning, the two sections of the turret were out of the driveway and onto the house. Maggie had helped. In September, we spent a couple of afternoons in the garage, cutting cedar shingles into uniform widths. At first Maggie did the sorting and I the cutting, but she wanted to get on the power saw, of course. She was pretty bored by the job, but, as always, was happy to make some money. So, as we raised the turret, I was happy that she had had a small part in it.

Many people came to see the turret lift. Jim's old friends, Pete and Tina, were here, and after everyone else left, they came inside for a visit. I offered to take Tina upstairs to look around and she was hesitant. Their son Ted lived with Jim for awhile a few years ago; Ted died last summer. Ted's old room is now my office. Entering this space was an invitation to Tina to go into the pain. I felt it and just stood close as she cried. I remembered returning in December to the room that Maggie had slept in when we were in England over the summer—how that had sucked the air right out of me. I'm glad Tina gave me a little bit of Ted today and that we could share our mothers' grief.

February 12

But I Talked So Much about Beth

Robbie, my dear friend from grad school, is here for a couple of nights, having come to DC for a meeting and some lobbying visits. I told her about this writing that I've been doing and offered to read her a couple of entries. I was very touched and pleased that she asked if she could read more and then stayed up late, reading every one. While I have shared a few of these with select people, no one has read them all.

Robbie was very solicitous, saying, "I had no idea how hard all of this is for you. I shouldn't have come. It was too much to ask you to have company. And last night I talked so much about Beth. I feel terrible." I was quick to tell her that, on the contrary, I am happy to have her with me, that her company requires little effort, and that I especially love hearing about her daughter. I realize there is some risk to writing about grieving. These snippets distill the experience down for someone who is reading, eliminating the stuffing of life that makes all of this bearable. Who could survive if in the wake of terrible loss we did not have the routines of daily life, the distractions of activity, and the solace of sleep to comfort us and dull the pain?

February 13

Numb

I went to the dentist to have a crown replaced. I am a small person and my dentists (and anyone else who has had to put me under) have always been amazed at how much local or general anesthetic it takes to affect me. Maybe this is part of the physical aspect of being an alcoholic and drug addict. I have never talked with my dentist about that, but Dr. Sehdev shot and shot into my gum and finally I felt numb, and then she shot again later to keep me numb.

I have always hated and loved that feeling. There is the relief from pain; I am happy not to feel the stab in the root, the scraping below the gum line, but there also is the strangeness of pressing a glass to my lips and not being sure that the seal is solid, putting a spoonful of soup into my mouth and only feeling it burn on one side. It is easy to believe that the other side is not burning. Then, slowly, the numbness wears off, and there is the simultaneous happiness that my face and mouth feel normal again and the cringe of awareness of the pain seeping in.

In the worst of my active alcoholism and drug abuse, shortly before I surrendered to the fact that I was hopelessly in the clutches of my disease, I saw a mother dropping her child off at the daycare center where I took Stephen. She had on a cap that said, "Comfortably Numb" and I thought, that is my motto, that is what I want, all the time.

I feel this strange fight now going on inside me. There is the impulse on the one hand to embrace life, the feeling that the worst insult I can do to Maggie and, by extension, to my God is not to be happy and active and delighted in my life. And there is the desire to escape, hide, protect myself, numb out because the pain of this loss can be so impossibly hard.

February 14

I See You Your Pain and Raise You a Dead Daughter

I'm not sure why, but there is the temptation to compare pain. Maybe when people tell me that their friend lost a child or that their beloved dog died recently, they really think that will help me. Maybe, once again, it's that people don't know what to say and want to say something that connects.

What makes me most uncomfortable is when I feel other people either silently or explicitly diminishing their own troubles because of mine, or, even worse, projecting that I am diminishing their troubles because of mine. On the other hand, if I am completely honest, I do sometimes think in response to someone else's complaints, *This is not a catastrophe.* There is the common use right now of "nightmare." For example, having to live in a really nice house in which your kitchen is being redone is not, I'm sorry, a "nightmare." But, when I can put that less tolerant part of me aside, I am increasingly coming to understand that pain is pain. Life hands us an array of really hard experiences to cope with: loss, disappointment, fear, depression, anxiety and physical pain, and whatever we are in at any given moment is what consumes our attention and energy; it feels really big.

February 15

Your Song

Jim and I flew to Las Vegas to see Elton John's show *The Red Piano* on Valentine's Day. It was a spur of the moment thing, a convergence of hearing that Elton John, whom I have always wanted to see perform, was on tour, knowing that the man isn't getting any younger, and having some airline miles to use before they expired. I am sure that there also is this need to keep moving, to be distracted. There also is the freedom of this first year of retirement, which delivers me the time to travel in ways I have never been able to do before. Finally, there is the sense that life is precious, that opportunities to live with gusto should not be passed up.

So, all of this brought us to the orchestra of the Coliseum at Caesar's Palace, watching Elton in his red suit, looking a little like Santa with his big belly, but still electric in his talent and his showmanship. I loved all of it, but the encore delivered me Maggie: "And you can tell everybody, this is your song. / It may be quite simple but, now that it's done,/ I hope you don't mind, I hope you don't mind / that I put down in words / how wonderful life is while you're in the world." How I cried to hear him sing those beautiful words and to know their truth! We don't think or say them enough.

February 16

Tinnitus

In the fall of 2002, Bill and I went to the symphony and, during the intermission I noticed that my ears were ringing. I thought it was some auditory reaction to the brass in the piece we had heard. But the ringing has never left. Sometimes I forget about it, at other times it is simply present, sometimes I am bothered and at its worst, it is disturbing enough to interfere with my life. I have been to the audiologist, I have had acupuncture, I have read up. It seems that this sudden and uninvited guest has become a permanent resident. Over the years, I have had to come to terms with this: to surrender and to accept that I will always have this sound with me as long as I live. I have come to call it "singing" in an effort to make it more pleasant.

Now, I have been slammed with another constant presence, another sudden and uninvited guest: mourning. There are many parallels, except that this time, I know from the start there will be no cure. There will be no miracle day when I wake up and realize that the noise of missing Maggie has disappeared.

February 17

Sex

Jim and I made love during the night after Maggie's death. I could not sleep and I reached for him, needing the intimacy and the release. Right through these first terrible months, I have been comforted by being able to lose myself, forget the pain, connect in love, revel in my alive body, laugh, and sometimes cry.

February 18

Facebook

We turned to Facebook immediately as a way of getting the word of Maggie's death out to the people whom we hadn't reached and also to let her friends know about the details of the plans for her memorial service and the fund in her memory. Because Maggie's email account was open on her computer, we were able to get a new password sent to that email, which gave us access to working on her Facebook profile. Very quickly Maggie's "wall" became a place where her young friends who were already on Facebook and the old fogeys who were just getting our feet wet could all read and write tributes and mourn together. One of the most poignant messages was from my cousin Sally's daughter, Emmy, who is just a few months older than Maggie:

> We shared a crib together and were at each other's first birthday parties when we were babies. We slid down your stairs on mattresses and got snow cones and had sleep-overs and played make believe in the woods when we were kids. We did plays together and played soccer and carpooled and experimented with

> make up in middle school. We went to dances and parties and dreamed about college and translated Latin when we were teenagers. You held my hand when I got a vaccination and helped me pick out a bed for my new apartment a few weeks ago. Why can't we experience life in our twenties as idealists trying to follow our dreams together? Why won't we be at each other's weddings? Why won't our babies share a crib? Why can't we complain about our aging bodies in our 40's? This is not the way things were supposed to happen! This is so unfair. I miss you. I'll miss you every day. I love you so much. I wish I had told you that more often.

As time has passed, the entries have become less frequent, but Bill and I have continued to use the wall as a place to post information or requests (the most recent from Janet, looking for photos for a scrap book she's making), and we log on as Maggie to accept friend requests or invitations (figuring that Maggie is definitely still going to all the parties). Maggie's friends and family have continued to write to Maggie periodically about grief or joy or memories or just about something in their lives they want to share with her. The most recent entry was from Maggie's dear friend, Jess, just checking in with her best valentine from her job at Disney World:

> happy VERY belated vday. the rents are down to visit--rab and tue will get to be up close and personal with giraffes as well as eat waffles

shaped like mickey mouse's head. it should be nice. finally put photos up in my room--u're the star of the show miss. LOVE ALWAYS

February 19

I am an Alive Girl

This morning I awoke remembering a dream. Maggie was very much alive, vibrant, lovely, happy, full, but I (in the dream) knew that she is dead and that this vision of her was the most extraordinary gift, a resurrection. And then lying in bed between sleep and activity, I was dwelling in the land of the dream and in the quiet blurred line between this world and the divine wherein I talk and live with God and Maggie and Daddy and Ganny. I felt the seduction of this place, how easy it would be to not make any effort at living. I felt a sort of dread at having to take on my alive body in the world. But dread is very close to dead.

Suddenly this line from a short story, "Ghost Girls" by Joyce Carol Oates came into my mind. In the story, a young girl, who has much to want to run away from in her troubled life, hears the sounds of girls playing under the porch. She crawls to find them and sees two sisters whom she is drawn to but whom she knows are ghosts. We feel her struggle, and then she says to them, "I am an alive girl." I never understood that struggle or that line before as I have this morning.

February 20

Guilt Reconsidered

Bill and I went to the Bereaved Parents group again. I shared about how I felt last time, but that, miraculously, I had wanted to come back. Bill talked also about his reactions to the meeting last time, but also about his guilt. Another father echoed: why had he not been home to drive his daughter? It is the father's job to protect his daughter. I could hear Bill's pain better in this stranger, accept the irrationality and know that the feeling is terribly real. A mother shared her guilt: why had she fallen asleep? Our leader said that guilt is something that all parents feel at some point around the death of their child, and I wonder: where is my guilt? I search my heart and honestly don't think that I have any guilt.

There is remorse. Bill had called me that morning to see if I could cover for him while he went to a meeting at church. I was on my way to Jim's farm and asked Bill if he could find someone else, which he did. If I had gone, I might have tried to awaken Maggie, surely would have gone into the room where she was sleeping and caressed her warm face and run my fingers through her tangled mop of hair. I might have lain down with her and felt her breath on my neck. I missed one last glimpse of my living, breathing daughter. But I would have left after Bill got home, and Maggie still would have died sometime later that afternoon. It is a blessing not to imagine that I could have saved her.

February 21

Heart Stones

One of the mothers at the Bereaved Parents group shared that twice when she has been desperate, despondent, truly unsure that she could go on, she has called out loud to her son, the first time begging, "Please, please help me, show me that you are with me," and the second time screaming into the wind at the beach. Both times, she has looked down to find stones in the shape of a heart. She passed them both around the circle and we each held these remarkable gifts. We each put our hands on these touchstones of her son's love. Of course I feel greedy, I want my own signs.

February 22

Sick

I am sick with a really bad cold. And I think, *Already I feel like I can't get out of bed in the morning and I want to make the pain go away; how can I be given something else that makes me feel like that?* I am old enough to know that there is no fairness in life. That good and bad are not parceled out in equal portion. I also do not believe that bad is punishment or good is reward. And, to complicate things even more, there is that twist where what seems like a bad thing turns out to have really good consequences. I remember a story I heard in which that keeps happening and the refrain is, "Good news, bad news, who knows?" But, all that said, it feels really shitty to be sick and in mourning simultaneously, and I'm sure that I can't find any good in it, at least right now. My only consolation is that Mom and I are leaving tomorrow for Florida; so maybe the sun will cure me.

February 23

Oscars

Kendal, Janet, Mom and I watched the Oscars. What is often a tedious and boring proposition was more pleasant because I was thinking about the movies that Maggie and I saw together: *Walle*, *Mamma Mia*, *Sex and the City*. We specialized in light romantic! But in every case, I remember the time as pure fun, even *Sex and the City*, which Maggie and I saw the day after a seizure episode so that she did not remember a thing about it. At the same time that I am savoring these memories, I am thinking that this is the last year I will have them. Next year, if I am silly enough to watch the Oscars, any movies I have seen will carry memories of other people. I worry about the slow whittling away of associations with my daughter, that my everyday life will be less and less about her. On the one hand I want to be less obsessed, but on the other, I don't want to lose her.

February 24

Mischelle

In 1974, in my first year of teaching, I became friends with an 8th grade girl to whom I taught English. She also was in my homeroom. I had had a charmed childhood and was distressed at all that Mischelle had to cope with in her family life. Later, after she left school and was placed in a girls' home, I became her Big Sister so that we could continue to see each other. We stayed in touch for awhile, but eventually lost contact. The last I'd heard, she was in Alaska.

Last week, totally out of the blue, she wrote me a message on Facebook, saying that she had been thinking about me very powerfully and continuously, so much so that she finally did the electronic legwork to find me. In the process, she learned about Maggie's death. She was distressed for me.

This distant reunion led to an actual physical reunion yesterday as she drove south and Mom and I drove north to meet her on Sanibel Island in Florida. As Mischelle strode across the parking lot, I knew her right away. There was the same spirit that had captured my heart thirty-five years ago. We walked at the nature sanctuary, loving the sun, the birds, and reconnecting after so many years. She told me that she named her own daughter after me, had called her Margaret, but that Margaret had begun to call herself Maggie. And that Maggie is a free spirit, a good hippy, just like mine. It was a linking of arms between two mothers who had both seen some pain but were still standing. How amazing that after all these years, someone to whom I had given hope would come do the same for me!

February 25

Trauma

I think about how over and over again, I have to reface the fact of Maggie's death. Every day I wrestle myself into this new life without my daughter, a life that doesn't fit, is not my choice. And it feels like trauma, new trauma every day. I worry, is this going to wear me down, change me into a person who carries life heavily or who is pessimistic or dead inside?

Joan Didion speaks of this possibility and it terrifies me. In *The Year of Magical Thinking*, she writes of what we have expected of death and grief: that people we love will die, that we will be in shock, "prostrate, inconsolable, crazy with loss," that the days closest to the death and the funeral will be the most difficult and that slowly we will move towards recovery of our sanity, health, and optimism. She says in fact that the funeral is "anodyne" (yes, I had to look that up too) and imbued with "the gravity and meaning of the occasion." And the truth, in contrast to our expectation, is that death creates an "unending absence that follows, the void, the very opposite of meaning, the relentless succession of moments during which we will confront the experience of meaninglessness itself" (189).

February 26

Family

I have accompanied my mother to Florida. We have escaped the cold, damp, windy mid-Atlantic to see my brother and his wife, who have no children of their own, and for whom Maggie was like a daughter. Among the four of us, there is much sharing of memories, and especially of photographs we have brought for Janet, because she wants to create an album in celebration of Maggie's life.

There are two photos that particularly tear me up: in the earliest, my brother is holding five-year old Maggie up as though they are dancing, but with Maggie facing out, both beaming, against the background of boardwalk skee ball machines, clearly winners! In the second, a very worn out, grown-up Maggie lies with her head in my brother's lap, still dressed in the black dress she wore to her grandfather's funeral, a day which began with a seizure. Kendal is looking down at her with such love and compassion, his fingers in her hair.

There is comfort for me in the bosom of my family, in the looks we exchange that speak our shared pain freely.

February 27

The Autopsy Report

Maggie's neurologist recently sent Bill and me the cover sheet of the autopsy report. It shows that Maggie had epilepsy and that there were signs of seizure activity around the time of death, but there is nothing more definite. I think about the moment of her death and feel very sure that it was a quick and painless release from her body. There are so many signs that point to Maggie's huge spirit being ready to be free of the physical form that had so limited it.

February 28

She Can Stay For as Long as She Needs to Stay

I told Janet a story about overhearing a woman talking on her cell phone and complaining about her daughter moving back in with her after graduating from college. It had taken a lot of work for me not to rip that Blue Tooth off her ear and say, "Be grateful for every day you have with your precious daughter."

Janet smiled and then relayed her own story of a colleague whose daughter decided to move back in with her for a few months to save money to buy a house. The daughter had not been the easiest child to deal with growing up and the few months had stretched into a longer time. When Janet asked her colleague how it was going, her friend smiled and said, "It's fine, it's really fine. You know, I think of your Maggie often, and I tell my daughter she can stay for as long as she needs to stay."

I know that when Maggie returned from college to live with me, even for short periods of time, I too complained to my friends about her shoes and clothes all over the place, and her dirty dishes and late hours and erratic eating habits.

I sometimes took Maggie for granted, sometimes resented it when her needs impinged on my life, but I would give anything to have those problems again.

March 1

Nimrod

To celebrate my homecoming, Jim and I went to the Baltimore Symphony last night. Among the pieces on the program was Sir Edward Elgar's *Enigma Variations*. The only one of the fourteen variations with which I was familiar was the ninth, "Nimrod," which Elgar wrote to embody August Jaeger, his publisher and dear friend. The piece begins with two intertwined harmonic lines played by the strings, then rises in volume with the addition of the horns. It is a slow and rhythmic building, which then fades to highlight a single clarinet, before rising slowly to a final crescendo of strings, horns, and drums. The piece ends with a gentle sigh. I have not done it justice in words, but the music is simple and beautiful, noble and somehow both uplifting and sad. No one has discovered with authority what Elgar's "enigma" is, but perhaps this is part of it: that the most beautiful and rich moments of life are full of both joy and sorrow, indeed that those labels cease to have real meaning as one feeling builds, weaves, and blends into the other.

March 2

Missing

I missed Jim so much while I was in Florida: missed the rhythms of our day, missed showing him the beautiful sunset, having his advice about how to cook the pork tenderloin, missed his bad jokes, his easy rapport with my family, his comforting presence in our shared life, his warm body in our sleeping. But always there was the faith that I would see him again, that all that I was missing would return to me and indeed would grow in love.

Missing Maggie is different. We had not shared a daily life since the summer of 2006 when she lived with me and we worked together. I have long experienced the letting go and the missing that comes from the natural and entirely right evolution of the child becoming independent of her parents. This missing her in death is a cavernous feeling. It begins with the terrible absence of Maggie: that I can't see her in this moment, can't talk to her, can't send her a text and expect that she will get back to me, can't make plans for next week. And that gaping hole can quickly enlarge into the immenseness of the future, the foreverness of my life without my daughter. That is the emptiness that will quickly overwhelm me and indeed will overtake me if I dwell there.

March 3

Change

I have done so much traveling in these four months since Maggie died. I have had the time and means to do so, which is part of it. Some of the trips were already planned because of my new freedom in retirement, and some, such as the trip north to ski and see family, would have occurred in any case, but there is no doubt that since Maggie's death, I have kept moving. My dear friend Christine has the motto, "Feelings can't hit a moving target," and in the case of some other times in my life, my busy pace has been a successful defense. But not in this case, the overwhelming sadness of missing Maggie is with me always.

Whenever I have returned home from these trips, I have had a day or two of depression, fatigue, listlessness. Perhaps it is just that solid reality that no matter where I go, the return home will never again hold that feeling of completeness, that sigh, "I'm home." Because the home has an empty room.

Henry Wadsworth Longfellow wrote the sonnet "The Cross of Snow" in memory of his wife who died suddenly of burns. It concludes, "Such is the cross I wear upon my breast / These eighteen years, through all the changing scenes / And seasons, changeless since the day she died."

I understand completely this paradox: that through all the changes there is the unchanging loss, constant and heavy in my heart.

March 4

The Fight

Jim and I rarely fight. Recently, we have had two major disagreements, each ending in periods of not speaking to one another. The source of the problem seems to be my inability to separate feelings about Maggie's death from an event we're planning in order to raise money for her fund, and Jim's very strong feeling that emotions have no place in the process. I am not an extremely emotional person, but much about life right now feels fragile and out of control. It is very difficult for me to function in the simplest of situations without my emotions getting stirred up and this event is something that is closely linked to Maggie.

In another time, I would be better able to stand up to Jim and stronger about weathering the emotional divide that inevitably follows a dust-up, but right now I am so vulnerable. Jim has been my stalwart supporter and I need to have him in my corner.

March 5

Saying No

Today I have had to call Jim's and my friend Joe and tell him that we have to shelve the fundraiser concert we have begun planning to raise money for the Maggie Feiss Fund. It is not only the two fights that Jim and I have had about the event, it is also how fragile I have felt in the process of working out the early logistics. It has been too hard for me to separate the idea of celebrating and honoring Maggie on her birthday from the business of organizing an event to raise money for her fund. I feel both sad and relieved. I wanted to be able to do this, but I can't.

I hate reneging on a commitment; it is not how I was raised. There is a Grimms' fairy tale called *The Frog Prince* in which a princess promises to be the frog's friend if he retrieves her golden ball from the pool. But when the frog appears at court, the princess rejects him. Her father insists that she allow the frog to sit beside her at the royal table, saying, "That which thou hast promised must thou perform." I loved this story as a child and asked my mother to read it to me frequently. Perhaps the lesson resonated because I already felt this sense of responsibility or perhaps, as Bruno Bettelheim suggests, my morality was shaped by the story.

In any case, I have carried this dictum all my life and have enacted it as the responsible eldest child, faithful wife, busy worker. Now, once again, I find that Maggie's death has altered my sense of myself.

March 6

Maggie's Possessions

Early on, two well meaning souls gathered up all of Maggie's things from Bill's apartment and took them to their house. I am sure they thought that he should not have reminders all around him, that they could save him from thinking about Maggie all the time. I got everything back as soon as we could manage it, and I have guarded Maggie's things rabidly, perhaps because touching, sorting, keeping and giving away the things that Maggie used, wore, bought, and loved has been one way I could feel like I was in control of what was happening. It has been a slow stripping away that I could manage.

Today I put one of the last packages in the mail. Maggie's Ultimate Frisbee teammates wanted one of her jerseys to carry with them and wear as a totem in their tournaments this spring. I sent the white shirt with the pink Hellions logo and Maggie's number, 1176, on the back and over the heart, to her teammate and roommate, Alice, aka Swift.

March 7

Seine

Yesterday I received an email from my dear friend and recovery sponsor, Mary Carol, who is spending the year teaching English in China. She has a student named Seine who would like to spend next year going to high school in the USA and is looking for a host family. I have never thought for a moment about such a thing, but the request piqued my interest. There is a big hole in me where a girl is supposed to be, and here is a young girl who needs a family. This morning, I still felt quite taken with the idea.

I don't know if this connection will come to pass, but thinking about it has made me feel very happy. The combination of that, a good long talk with Mary Carol this morning, a warm and beautiful day of working in the garden, and fun with our old neighbors, the Dyjak family, tonight, eating burgers and fries and watching a movie, have made for a great day.

March 8

You Don't Get to Choose Where Your Support Comes From

One of the things I talked with Mary Carol about was the feeling of disappointment and confusion and yes, to be honest, even resentment I have about a very close old friend whom I feel has not really been there for me. There are all sorts of reasons why this might be, and I have tried to rationalize my way out of the feelings, but I find them still there.

Mary Carol is so good. She listened well, asked a few questions, and then advised that I list all the things this friend has done for me for which I feel grateful. It is a long list. Finally she asked, "Are you getting the support you need from other people?" And I immediately said, "Yes, absolutely, unequivocally, yes." "Well, my dear, then you need to let this go. You don't get to choose where your support comes from." I knew immediately that this lesson was true and important. As long as I am writing the script for what someone is supposed to do or say to support me in my grief, then I risk two dangerous results. One I will have all those unpleasant feelings about that person not living up to my expectations, and two, I am likely to miss or fail to appreciate some of what is coming to me, unexpected, unearned, and unreciprocated, just as gifts.

March 9

I Didn't Get to Say Goodbye

Jim and I watched a kid's movie last night, the animated Disney/Pixar film, *Cars*. We had some good laughs and it was fun. As is true in many Disney movies, some unusual and unexpected friendships are formed, from which our hero learns some necessary life lessons. One of the most wonderful friends is the tow truck named Tow Mater. When Lightning, the hot shot race car, takes off in a hurry for California in order to be there in time for his big tie-breaker race, Tow Mater moans, "I didn't get to say goodbye." Before I knew it, I had tears welling up, which made me feel a little sheepish; this was, after all, an animated movie and the characters were . . . *cars*! But my reaction made me think: clearly I have some feeling about the suddenness of Maggie's death, about not having been there, about not having had a chance to say goodbye.

March 10

Chasm

An old friend and I had lunch together and she told me about her sister, whose son died in December, 2007, from alcoholism. Her sister comes every weekend to stay with her so as not to be alone. She describes the experience of living with her son's death as walking the edge of a chasm. I got a chill when my friend shared that, because it is the first image that has struck me as exactly right. There is this huge, gaping emptiness in my life. I am trying my best to walk beside it: keeping my balance, staying focused on life at the top rather than obsessing about the hole, holding the fear of falling at bay, but always the awareness of the space is right there.

March 11

Angry and Sad are a Bad Combination

Yesterday I was annoyed with Jim because he was being stubborn and, to my mind, getting involved with something that wasn't his to manage. Then I had some errands to run and he asked me to do a few things for him, which I agreed to. Those things did not go as smoothly as they could have and the traffic was bad, and for the hour I spent out and about, I got very wound up with anger and resentment. I was stoked when I walked back into the house and let Jim know it. Then I said, "Do you even know why I am annoyed at you?" to which he replied, "No, and I don't think I want to." Well, that was a stiff wind to the smoldering fire, and I blazed off and out the door. Thank God I didn't get behind the wheel.

I walked the streets like a crazy woman, having conversations with a person who wasn't there. I tried to settle down by going to the library, to the knitting store, by just walking, but by the time I was on my way home, almost two hours later, I was still raging. There is a new shop on Frederick Road, opened by a very sweet woman who makes handbags. About a month ago, I had stopped into this bright, cheerful shop to introduce myself and check out her wares. Jonna was so kind and personable, and her bags were so Maggie: hip, clever, colorful, that I found myself telling her about my daughter and her death. In turn, Jonna told me that she had lost her first husband suddenly and how difficult mourning his death had been for her.

So, there I was, on my way home last night and still in trouble, when Jonna came out of her shop and saw me. "Great bag," she called, referring to my knitting bag. "A friend of mine made it for me," I replied, simultaneously feeling like someone had lassoed me and that I was being drawn back to the shop. "You don't look so good," Jonna said as I got closer. I choked out, "Angry and sad are a bad combination," and as I said the words, the tears came. I hadn't known I was sad. I reminded her that I was the person who had lost her daughter, and we talked about prayer being the only path out of this kind of pain. Jonna said, "I will pray for you. I am a prayer warrior. You come into the shop any time you need a place to be safe."

Once the tears began, then I couldn't stop them. I had had no idea the degree to which I had been using the anger to protect against the sadness. I came home, tried to read, tried to do yoga, tried to pray, but finally I just had to crawl into bed and pull the covers over my head, curl into a fetal ball and sob and moan and beat the pillow. I was in free fall. Jim did not come to me. Finally, I felt completely drained; I lay flat on my back in bed and sort of drifted. I heard Jim call upstairs, "Meg, dinner is ready." I didn't want to eat but I washed my face and came down. Jim hugged me and sat me down and put a plate of delicious food in front of me and said, "Eat your spinach."

This morning, I have sufficient distance and presence of

mind to thank my beloved for not jumping out of his perfectly good airplane without a parachute so that he could "save" me. We didn't both need to be in free fall. He was there to cushion my landing. I also am going to stop by Jonna's shop to thank her and tell her I'll be back.

March 12

A Lifetime

Over the years, people have recommended the book *Many Lives, Many Masters* by Dr. Brian Weiss, but I tend to steer away from popular psychology and theology. Nonetheless, recently I have felt drawn to read it, and I found it at the library. I like Weiss's scientific skepticism about what was happening as his patient unveiled her past lives under hypnosis, and I understand how the experience of treating Catherine was life changing for him, both as a psychiatrist and as a person. But I didn't need to be convinced about past lives. I always have believed in a soul; I think it is what God is, all the accumulated souls. It also is really hard for me to believe that a soul only gets one chance to try on a body and to learn from life.

After I moved out when Bill and I separated, it was very hard to face that our marriage was ending. I was searching for help and guidance in many directions, one of which was to meet with a psychic. Anat said to me, "It is hard for you to let go because you still have powerful ties to Bill. You feel that you have more work to do together, and you do, but that work does not all have to be done in this lifetime." There was something comforting about that idea. Clearly, Bill and

I have souls that are deeply entwined. I expect we will have many more lives in which to understand everything we have to teach each other.

Now I hold onto these ideas I've developed about life and death, not only believing that Maggie is with the other spirits, free of her physical body and its failings, but also that she and I will surely be two souls who pass each others' way again, and that part of the purpose of her death is to teach me something about my life. It is a distant and rather abstract comfort, but I'll take it.

March 13

Contact

I was not as taken with *Many Lives, Many Masters* as many people were, but I was interested. One of the notions that intrigued me was revealed to Weiss through Catherine about contact between the spiritual and physical states. Weiss asks, "How do you make contact? How does the message come through?" Catherine replies, "Sometimes you can appear before that person . . . and look the same way you did when you were here. Other times you just make a mental contact. Sometimes the messages are cryptic, but most often the person knows what it pertains to. They understand. It's mind-to-mind contact" (141).

I have such strong feelings of Maggie, particularly just after waking. I love lying in bed, warm and relaxed, and communing with her. I have not often received any messages, it's just a comforting feeling of love and protection, like being held and rocked must be for a baby.

March 14

My Epilepsy is a Burden

Shortly after Maggie had her first seizure at age eleven, I witnessed one of my students having what I thought might be a seizure in my class. He did not fall on the floor in a fit of spasms, which is what most people think of as a seizure; my student simply smacked his hand against the desk several times. If I had not been educated about different kinds of seizures because of Maggie, I probably would have written it off as goofy, 10th grade boy behavior. Instead, I spoke to my student after class and told him that I was concerned enough about his action that he needed to see his doctor. He had a brain tumor. Within a week, he was undergoing brain surgery and then months and months of intense therapy to get his brain working right again, but he is fine.

Of course I told Maggie, and her first response was, "Maybe that's why I needed to have epilepsy, Mom, so that you could save your student's life." True, Maggie had a flair for the dramatic, but the idea was certainly some comfort for all of us during those first years of adjusting to the hard facts of Maggie's disease.

Maggie had such big dreams for her life after college: she was going to travel the world, live in New York or Boston or San Francisco and get some work and life experience, then she was going to "come back and fix Baltimore." But her seizures had become so debilitating and the drugs she was taking had so compromised her thinking that she was unable to travel or get a job or even live away from home. This girl who had always lived so fully was feeling her options constrict. We all were beginning to see the possible real limitations to her life as an adult with serious epilepsy.

It was at the end of August, when Maggie was still on the drug, Topamax, and really at the nadir of her health. Maggie was spending the night with me at my apartment, and we were having a talk about some of her options. She broke down crying. "I just want to be away from home, living with my friends, working, having a life." I said that we all wanted that for her, and that I was sure, eventually, it would happen. "What is stopping you?" I asked. She was quiet for awhile; I remember her sad face as she said, "I feel like my epilepsy is such a burden." I think I responded with something lame about all of us having struggles and this was hers, but inside I felt myself constrict. This was not a side of Maggie I had ever seen; I felt at that moment like she was giving up the fight.

I don't know what to make of this now. At the time of her death, Maggie was off that drug and she was thinking more clearly. She had started a rigorous diet, which had slowed down the seizure activity. She was losing weight, exercising, and generally feeling much better. She had found a job, quite unexpectedly, and was due to start it the day after she died. She had every reason to be hopeful. But was there also a part of her that had felt her life as an adult with epilepsy and was crumbling under the weight of it?

March 15

Ides of March

I met Bill forty-one years ago today. We were both at my friend Mallory's birthday party, I by invitation, he by charm. I loved him right away, knew in some way that our lives together were bound to be. I am thankful to reflect on all this today and not to feel the tearing anger, sadness, loss and regret that plagued the early years of our separation. I realize that Maggie's death has catapulted us into a more gracious and compassionate place. We were getting there, but now, anything less would be destructive and cruel.

March 16

"Terps Are In"

This morning's headline in *The Sun* read: "Terps Are In!" College basketball was Maggie's first sports addiction. Before she became a passionate USC Trojan football fan, she loved March madness. During high school, she would invite her girlfriends to crunch into our narrow den to sit all over each other and watch the Maryland Terrapins play.

Maggie and I were in Amsterdam in the spring of 2002 when the Terps won the NCAA championship. When we came downstairs to breakfast in our hotel, Maggie raced to the gift shop to find a paper and there, on the front page of the *International Herald Tribune*, was the news. She shrieked, ran around the lobby waving the paper, and then had to have conversations about it with everyone in the restaurant, and if they weren't Americans and did not know what she was talking about, she explained how important this accomplishment was.

I never shared Maggie's love for the sport, but our whole family adored her passion. So now we are looking at our first NCAA tournament without our girl. Stephen and Bill will argue about their brackets, gloat over wins and pine over losses; even I will watch a Terps game or, if we're lucky, two, but it will all be a bit flat, because Maggie won't be here, cranking it all up.

March 17

Family Secrets

I ran into someone I used to know well but haven't seen in years. He had heard about Maggie's death and was full of sympathy. Then he told me about his own daughter who has recently returned home to live with him and his wife. My old friend confided that his daughter had finally found the courage to leave her physically abusive husband. Knowing that I am a writer, he asked if he could send me something his daughter had written about her experience; I said of course. The piece arrived yesterday and I read it with fascination and horror. This was a smart, capable, young woman whom I had known when she was a child. She did not fit my idea of the kind of woman who stays with a man who beats her, and her parents are not my profile of the sort of people who have to save their daughter from such a life. All my prejudices and misconceptions were right in my face, along with the reality that this could happen to anyone. Right beside that realization was the thought that my great pain as a parent is out there—almost everyone knows my daughter died. If someone doesn't know, there is no shame in telling them. Sympathy and comfort are readily available to me as I walk through this ordeal. Other family tragedies are less public and therefore, to my mind, the pain may be even more intense because it is not as readily shared.

March 18

Ginger Tea

Anne Marie sent me a little package. It was a box of ginger tea with a note: "I like this new tea; hope you enjoy it too." Annie knows ginger tea is my favorite, especially in winter when I need to be warmed all the time. My father loved ginger too. Candied ginger was one of his special treats. A gesture like this is priceless; it says—I'm thinking of you, I want to do something to comfort you, I love you.

March 19

Lonely

Last night Bill and I went to our third Bereaved Parents meeting. Each time gets a little less scary as I come to know these other parents and their deceased children. Their pain feels less raw and intrusive to me, more a part of them as people I care about and therefore want to help and share with.

One father talked about his loneliness and I was struck by that word. I haven't thought about how Maggie's death has left me feeling lonely but there is certainly that: a place in me where Maggie is supposed to be which feels empty and lonely. There is also the loneliness of so few other people understanding what I'm going through and the uncertainty of how much to say about Maggie and her death and my grief before it is too much.

March 20

Anat

On the night of Maggie's death, I slept fitfully. Many thoughts jumped in my head, among them was Anat, a very gifted psychic whom I have seen three other times at critical junctures in my life. I knew that Maggie was telling me that I could reach her through Anat.

I wasn't ready until now, but this morning, I saw her. When Anat greeted me, I knew that she did not know and had not heard about Maggie's death. She was cheerful and chatty about her new office décor. As we settled down and she was putting the make-up on my palms as she always does so as to better see the lines, she said, "You have come here with questions, you want to know about relationships, work, there are some health issues." These were all true, but would be of anyone in mid-life; I knew she was just finding her balance so I said, "You'll get it, Anat." Then she held my hands and was quiet, she sighed and I could feel her energy shifting, and then she said, "The last four months have been very difficult for you, you are grieving, deeply, someone very close to you has died. Who is this person, a woman, not your mother, but your heart is breaking and you are not sure that you can bear it." I was crying. "Who is this who died?" she asked and I choked out, "My daughter, Maggie."

Anat shifted again, she was back, just another woman in the room with someone she cares about who was in pain. She looked at me deeply and hugged me, "Oh Meg, I am so sorry. That is terrible." I told her nothing, just let the tears fall. We reentered the session with a different feel. There was an intensity, almost an urgency; I felt her gratitude for the gift that would enable her to help me.

My hour stretched into an hour and a half, and Anat told me so many things. There is much that is completely true and much that I don't understand yet. I have absolute trust in her ability to know things beyond the physical world. I cried almost all the way through our time together and came home so depleted, like I had done a huge amount of work. I know Anat felt the same.

March 21

Death Valley & Death

Mom, Jim, and I planned this trip to Death Valley long before Maggie died. It is a funny story actually. In the spring of '08, we invited Mom to join us for a Smithsonian Journeys tour to Panama, a place she has always wanted to go, scheduled for fall '09. Mom responded, "I can't possibly plan that trip, I could be dead by then." "Okay, Mom," I answered, "I'll try to find something sooner, like next spring, how about March, will you still be alive in March?" So I searched the Smithsonian Journeys website for a trip in a warm climate with a nature focus and some hiking. The result: Death Valley. I called Mom and said, "We've got you covered either way."

And so here is one more piece in this inexplicable puzzle, which makes some kind of crazy sense. Several other people on this trip have suffered the death of someone very close in the past year; there are two widows and one woman my age whose best friend died. I feel an amazing calm in Death Valley, despite the fact that it is the site of much "recent" geological activity. Nothing is busy. The landscape is barren. The light is uninterrupted by clouds or trees or humidity and it illuminates with a clarity and intensity I have never seen before. Everything is big and open and slow. There is incredible subtle beauty: the ways water has carved rock and wind has sculpted sand, the varieties of rock layered into a story of the long geologic past, the strange colors of the mineral-rich volcanic rock. There are none of the sensory stimuli I am accustomed to and perhaps in their absence, I have the feeling that this valley is a safe place into which to pour my immense grief.

I think there is more to the name than the legendary westward settler who turned her back on the site where one of her party died and said, "Good-bye Death Valley." Would the name have stuck if there were not something else here that says: this is a place that can hold the grief that accompanies death?

Meg Tipper

March 22

Geologic Time

We have a geologist with us in Death Valley, Kirt Kempter from Santa Fe. He is the perfect guide to the rocks while we are out on our walks and he also gives great lectures in the evenings. One of my gifts from this desert is what Kirt calls, "geologic time." I had never heard the expression but it goes something like this: "These tectonic shifts occurred within the past 500 thousand years, very recent geologic time."

Kirt also told us about the calendar year metaphor, which helps me understand these numbers. Planet earth is 4 1/2 billion years old. If we just take the last half billion years and turn that into a calendar year, the dinosaurs would have appeared in August and disappeared in mid-November (actually Kirt had the exact date, but I don't remember it). Man, homo sapiens, has been on the planet for the last hour of the year, about 11:00pm on December 31.

For this student of literature, who has thought of Homer as ancient, suddenly three thousand years just isn't very impressive. And for this selfish human being, who can get wound very tightly in the vicissitudes of life and particularly right now in the immensity of mourning, this new scale of time is a healthy pulling back and loosening.

March 23

Stone in the Wall

Mom told me that when she was on a trip to the Grand Canyon, her guide advised that each of them take a moment to find a special stone and take a quiet moment to place it in a crevasse of the canyon wall in memory of a loved one. When we were in Titus Canyon today, we both did so. My rock was small, triangular and pink. I rubbed it with my spit to make the colors come up, held it in my hand while I said a blessing for Maggie and felt gratitude for her life, and then I placed it in a nook of amazing limestone, according to Kirt, about 800 million years old.

I felt so peaceful after that and immediately began to notice many such places where small rocks rested in places where they couldn't have fallen naturally. It was a wailing wall and the spirits were everywhere.

March 24

Purple and Yellow Flowers

Anat told me that Maggie wanted me to have purple and yellow flowers. I thought, *That's crazy, I am not going to spend money on cut flowers when I am about to leave town; I'll get some when I get back.* Ever practical. Later I went to the hardware store to get a watering can so that our tenant, Carolyn, could take care of my little seedlings while we were away. In front of the garden department was a mass of purple and yellow pansies. I laughed and said out loud, "Okay, okay, you win!" I bought three beautiful plants, and Jim put them in the ground right next to the front steps to greet us every time we come home.

Mom came over that night to be ready to leave early the following morning. In her room is a photo I took of Maggie and her in 2002 when we visited Florence together. We were looking at the picture closely, remembering the day, the sweetness of Mom's nuzzle into Maggie's neck, trying to recall what they were being silly about, and then we noticed something I'd never seen before: purple and yellow pansies in the planter behind them.

Then, today, as we drove in Death Valley, so barren of vegetation and any signs of life in this land of less than two inches of rain a year, along the road, where a bit of run-off makes for a more concentrated rainfall, we saw clusters of wildflowers, and yes, they were purple and yellow.

March 25

Babies

Today on our walk, I saw a mother sitting with her infant in the shade of a boulder. I have gravitated to babies since Maggie died, as I did to this little one. Safe in his mother's arms, he looked at me with complete trust and love. He met my eyes steadily, and I drank in his connection with the divine. Sometimes I can feel Maggie looking out of the eyes of babies so strongly that it makes me cry.

March 26

Bird & Butterflies

There is very little life in Death Valley. It is an inhospitable climate for plants and animals. Nonetheless, there have been several times during our trip when I became aware of wildlife hanging out near me. When we were on the edge of the Ubehebe Crater, the wind shot up from the inside so wildly I had to put my hat back in the van. As I stood, taking in the grandeur of this volcanic crater, I saw hovering there, just over the edge, a bird of prey. He was using the updraft to float there: he about 500 feet up and I on the ground, side by side. He stayed there with me for a full minute before we both peeled off. Another time, I was sitting in the back of the van by myself. As we pulled away from the canyon where we had been hiking, several little butterflies cavorted along beside my window for quite awhile.

It comforts me to see these moments as little visitations from Maggie, her reminder to me to notice beauty, to stop and feel majesty, to play, and to enjoy being alive. There is also no denying the cynical side of me that says this is sentimental wishful thinking.

March 27

Dawn

We awoke early and gathered with other hearty folks, bundled against the wind and the cool desert night, to stand at Zabriskie Point to watch the sun light up the distant mountains and Badlands. There we were, waiting, not facing east where the sky was lightening, but focused to the west where the sun would first hit. The glow caught the peaks, then crawled remarkably quickly down the slopes, then began to illuminate the hills closer to us with that gold of rising and setting suns. Slowly, we watchers began to leave; the day had begun.

I thought about our absolute faith that the sun would come up. Not faith, but scientific knowledge that the sun is not moving at all, but rather the earth, and that that spinning will not suddenly stop. But the world does stop, one morning the dawn as we have come to expect it for, say, twenty-two years does not come, and we have to figure out how to light up the day without it.

March 28

Love

When Maggie turned twenty-one, Bill and I gave her a trip to Las Vegas. Her friend Jess flew out from Boston to meet her. They stayed at the Flamingo Hotel, and we gave them tickets to see *Love*, the Cirque de Soleil performance that is set to Beatles music. Stephen had given Maggie the CD for Christmas, the perfect gift for someone who had been passionate about the Beatles since she was eight years old. Maggie and Jess were crazy about the show, so much so that Maggie went back and saw it again with her friends Rex and Bambi.

So, of course, during this visit in Vegas with Mom before returning home, we had to see *Love*, which I hoped might redeem the whole excessive experience. The show started slowly, and I thought I might be disappointed, having seen *Ka*, which began so explosively with the ship tossed in the storm. But the show came together and built in intensity, just as the Beatles' career did. And it was magic, sheer magic, and absolutely full of Maggie. I could not stop thinking about her being there, seeing the show, and loving it. There were two scenes that vied for my favorites: Lucy in the Sky with Diamonds and Octopus's Garden. They were similar in that there was amazing trapeze work with stunning, but simple visual effects. Lucy hung in the star-glittering sky, dressed in white, and doing the most breath-taking rope acrobatics against the darkness. In the Octopus's Garden, the dark space was transformed from sky to sea with the white octopus and white jellyfish bouncing and twisting on their ropes. I couldn't stop smiling.

And the tears finally came: "All you need is love," one of the songs Stephen chose to play at Maggie's memorial service, was the finale: an explosion of colored lights, confetti, characters, costumes, and the audience singing.

March 29

Francine

On our last night in Las Vegas, we saw the show *Jersey Boys* about the rock and roll group Frankie Valli and The Four Seasons. Unlike *Love*, which I knew would be packed full of associations with Maggie, I was not prepared for anything in this play to be a trigger. After all, this was music from my early youth, the 1960s, way before Maggie's life and never on her radar.

But then, suddenly in the play, amid all the turmoil of a life on the road, a disintegrated marriage, an alienated family, Frankie gets a call that his daughter, Francine, is in the ER, and he rushes there only to be handed a box of her belongings; she is dead of a heroine overdose. Later, when an old friend approaches with condolences and asks, "How old was she?," I knew that the answer was going to be twenty-two. Mom, sitting beside me, gasped. Later she told me that she too knew. Frankie is devastated. The priest comes, puts his hand on Frankie's shoulder, and says, "Don't blame yourself." Frankie says, "Who else is there to blame?"

March 30

Swamped and Disconnected

I have just finished reading Mary Lawson's lovely book *Crow Lake*. There are many losses grieved in this story, and I was touched by several apt descriptions. At age seven, the narrator and main character, Kate, loses both her parents in a car accident. She says, "I remember Matt talking to me . . . and I remember the enormous effort required to even hear what he said. I was so swamped by unmanageable emotions that I couldn't feel a thing. It was like being at the bottom of the sea" (53).

Later in the book, Kate deals with another wrenching and abrupt change in her sense of the world. Afterwards she reluctantly attends a party: "I would like to be able to say that I threw myself into the spirit of it all, but the truth is, I still felt a bit dazed. A bit abstracted. It's going to take time, I guess. If you've thought in a certain way for many years, if you've had a picture in your mind of how things are and that picture is suddenly shown to be faulty, well, it stands to reason that it will take a while to adjust. And during that time, you're bound to feel . . . disconnected. Anyway, that was how I felt—and still feel, to some degree. What I would really have liked to do was sit quietly somewhere, preferably under a tree, and watch the goings-on from a distance" (290). I know this feeling precisely and have been thinking about it more lately, about how my whole picture is changed and how disconnected I feel from it, about how I often want to watch my life rather than really participate so that I can come to see myself in it in a way that makes sense and feels real.

March 31

The Past

I awoke this morning thinking about something that hadn't really occurred to me before. I have been very clear about how the present and future have changed irrevocably because of Maggie's death. But today I thought about the past and realized that even the past is changed because now it has a different weight. If value is determined by supply and demand, then my memories of life with Maggie have just rocketed in value. So my feelings about the past are different, and I am afraid that I also will distort the memory, change the past with my beliefs about who Maggie was, who I was, and how I want to remember it all. I don't want to do that. I want her life to be real and true.

April 1

Macy's Support Team

My old friend, Diane, has been sending me cash donations for Maggie's Fund along with a short note. It is a pep rally every time one comes. Diane gets a small bonus whenever she signs up a customer for a Macy's credit card; she matches it and then donates. Today I received another note and contribution, but this time, there was more money. Some of Diane's co-workers have joined her; she said they are finding it rewarding to give to Maggie's Fund. This kind of on-going, thoughtful, and generous support helps me so much. It is hard to be down about my life when there are such kind people in it.

April 2

Ask Ali

From Facebook:

Hey Ali,

I am Maggie Feiss's Mom. Please accept my friend request, I want to ask you about something.

Cheers, Meg

March 23 at 10:48am
Hi Meg,

I just confirmed you. I met you at Maggie's memorial and a few other times when you were visiting in LA. What can I help with?

Ali

April 1 at 7:36pm
Hey Ali,

Of course I remember you and was so touched that you came in November, just wanted to make sure that you knew who I was!

I went to see a psychic a few weeks ago and one of the things I asked her was whether Maggie was okay with me reading her journals. She said that Maggie said yes and that much would be revealed about what was really going on with her feelings about her Dad's and my separation. Then the psychic said that Maggie told her to tell me to ask Ali if I wanted to know more. You are her only friend named Ali. Does this make sense to you? Did you all talk about this? I'm not asking you to tell me what Maggie said if you did; I just thought it was interesting!

I hope you are doing well. I miss Maggie like crazy, but somehow life is bearable one day at a time and sometimes even joyful.

Sending love, Meg

Today at 12:19pm
Hi Meg,

That is so weird. Maggie and I talked a lot about your separation. I can't believe that the psychic would say that! We talked mainly during freshman year, and a lot of the time she was really upset. I don't really remember a lot of the conversations, only that it was a topic a lot of the time. I still can't believe that she said that! It's so weird! I have vivid

> memories of being in her dorm room talking. She would sit at her computer and I would sit on a little bench or something and we would chat about it. Sometimes she would make me eat peanut butter and banana sandwiches with her.
>
> I miss Maggie a lot as well - I honestly do not even know how you are being so strong. I think about her a lot too. She made such an impact on so many people - we are all so honored to have known her.
>
> I hope you have a great summer. I am moving to DC in May, so I hope that one day we will cross paths again.

So, once again, Anat amazed me, hit another one out of the park. That Maggie was very troubled about our separation is no news to me, but that she spent time sharing with Ali is, and it makes me so happy. Maggie was a very private person and she did not like to be needy. She went to one therapy session each with two different counselors during the separation but was very disdainful of that way of coping. I knew she wrote in her journal, I knew she got mad at me and cried, but I am so glad that she found a comforting ear in Ali during that very difficult freshman year.

April 3

Rex and Bambi and Hellions

Maggie made such good friends on her Ultimate Frisbee team at USC, but whenever she talked to us about them, she called them by their Ultimate nicknames. Maggie's name was Box. It began with the idea of Pandora's Box because Maggie had a big mouth and all kinds of things would come out. First they tried Pandora, but that didn't really suit her; Box was perfect!

The second time Maggie saw *Love*, it was with two of those friends, Rex and Bambi. I wanted to write them about seeing the show and thinking about them and Maggie, but of course, I needed to find out their real names. I contacted Maggie's former teammate Stephanie (Fonda) on Facebook, who told me Bambi and Rex's real names but also that they broke up a few months ago. There was this moment of powerful disconnect. In Maggie's world, the one she still inhabits in my mind, Rex and Bambi are a couple whom she loves, whom she does fun things with. I felt really sad and upset and I was not sure why.

Stephanie also added the following, "I actually got to see them [Rex and Bambi] this past weekend! The Hellions played a tournament in Austin and I drove up. We brought out Maggie's jersey and Rex played in it for a few points. I know Maggie was with us screaming "Hellions! Hell Yeah!"

That made me smile. Maggie is so strongly with me all the time, and it is comforting to know that others are feeling her, invoking her spirit, taking strength.

April 4

Posthumous Award

Dear Meg,

On behalf of Bryn Mawr's Alumnae Board, I would like to inform you that your daughter Maggie has been named the recipient of the 2009 Young Alumnae Award. Award winners are selected by an alumnae board committee, and this award is given to "an alumna who has graduated within the last 20 years and who has distinguished herself in the community or in her profession." Maggie's enthusiasm for helping others, exemplified by her work with Relay for Life, the Enterprise Foundation, and her volunteer work at local schools earned her this honor. It is no surprise to us that a young woman who won the Alumnae Association Award on Class Day would be awarded another such tribute. We only wish she could be here to receive it herself.

This letter came in the mail recently. Of course I cried but I also felt so proud. I know how amazing Maggie was, but it is always nice when I get the confirmation that others know it too. I received a card recently with a picture of Jackie Robinson and his words, "A life is not important except in the impact it has on others." I remember so many people making a point to tell me in the weeks following Maggie's memorial service how they felt inspired by her life, how they wanted to do more for others.

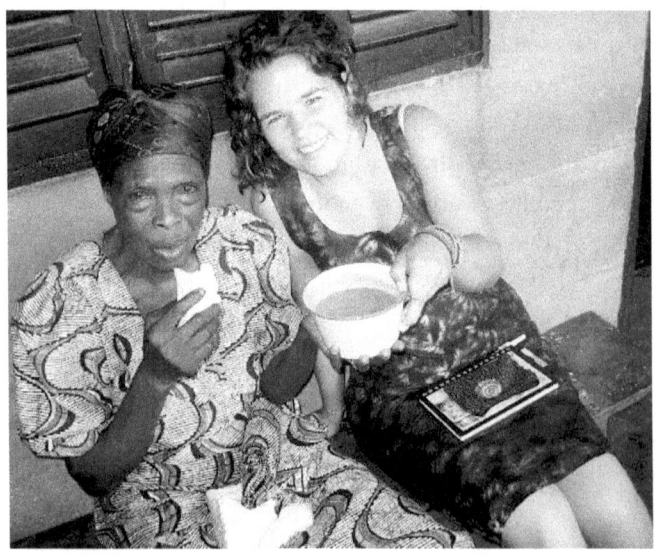

April 5

Tatyana

We tried so many different medications to combat Maggie's seizures, but last summer, nothing was working well. In addition, Maggie was mugged in July when she was in Barcelona with her friend Alex Pelly, and that experience had been traumatic for both of them. When I spoke to Maggie afterwards, she said, "I need therapy." She had never said that to me before. We talked with Maggie's neurologist about trying acupuncture as an alternative treatment, both physical and emotional, and he was supportive. One of my dear friends suggested a practitioner who put us in contact with "the perfect person." Tatyana Maltseva was a neurologist in the Ukraine before she came to the US and became an acupuncturist. She knew both sides of the disease.

She and Maggie loved each other. Maggie was her daughter's age and reminded Tatyana of her. Maggie always came away from her sessions with Tatyana with a glow, a heightened energy, and a loving spirit. One day, we stopped for coffee afterwards and they were giving away free samples of some sinful concoction. At first I declined and Maggie looked at me in that way only she could and said, "You will drink this!" (She was on her diet and couldn't.) I took a sip and said, "Oh my God, it's heaven." Then she turned to the other customers, most of whom were older, thin women with shopping bags, and said in her commanding voice: "Unless you have diabetes or some other medical condition, you MUST try this drink!"

The last time Jim and I saw Maggie, she and Bill had stopped at our house after coming from acupuncture. Maggie had that characteristic post-acupuncture lightness, and she seemed so happy. It was a beautiful day. Jim has told me that he felt that Maggie was more loving towards him that day, that he felt a kind of acceptance and even affection from her that he had never felt before.

Tatyana had only known Maggie for a few months, but she came to the memorial service and waited in the long line to comfort us at the reception. She was crying, and I know she felt the loss very powerfully. At the time, she asked me to send her a photograph of Maggie as she did not have one. I have finally taken the time to do that today, feeling grateful for all she was able to do to open and heal my sweet girl before she died.

April 6

Mahler's Ninth

Jim and I heard the Baltimore Symphony Orchestra perform Mahler's Ninth Symphony yesterday. I was not familiar with it and found it very powerful. I learned from the program and from the question and answer session held by our amazing conductor, Marin Alsop, that Mahler faced the deaths of many loved ones during his lifetime. Just before he began composing the ninth, his beloved daughter died suddenly. Knowing this, I listened for her. The work, composed near the end of Mahler's life, has many overtones of death, but I was sure that one moment when the flutes and piccolo share a very magical interlude, that Mahler's little four year old daughter had inspired him. I asked Alsop if she interpreted any particular part of the symphony as having been influenced by that recent, tragic loss, and she fluttered her expressive hands and said, "Those angelic flutes in the third movement." I felt so happy to have heard it.

April 7

Purgatory

Someone I do not know well learned of Maggie's death. After offering condolences, she asked, "Was she Catholic?" And when I said no, she looked stricken, shook her head, and said, "Then she's in purgatory."

Was this some kind of sick joke? When I told my friend John, who comes from a big Catholic family, about this encounter, he suggested that I pray for the person who said that. It seems like a good idea, but I'm not sure I'm feeling that spiritually generous.

April 8

Love and Prayer

Helen and I talked with Chris Warner when we were climbing today. Chris is the founder of Earth Treks Climbing Centers in the Mid-Atlantic area, mountaineering guide, author, leadership trainer, husband, father and all around good guy. As we talked, I opened up about Maggie's death, and Chris related several experiences he has had of being with people when they died. In one case, he was giving CPR to a young man, who had been electrocuted. Chris said, "I had my hands on his chest, and I felt his soul leave his body." Another time Chris was bracing the head of an older man who was trapped in his car after a crash. "I felt his pulse stop. And at moments like this, you just have to pour all your love into this person, this stranger." Climbing K-2, Chris and his team had their sights on a man who was trapped and dying but whom they couldn't reach to save. Chris was in contact with the family and he said, "Just get everyone to pray. Send him your love and your prayers. It is all you can do." The man died, but I told Chris, "The prayers help. I know. As one who has been carried by prayer, I know. You couldn't save him, but you helped him. You helped the family too."

April 9

Knitting

Yesterday when I saw Chris, he asked me what I had been doing with myself since my retirement. I said traveling, reading, writing, rock climbing, and a lot of knitting. He looked at me funny about the knitting. I don't think Jim really gets the knitting either, he wonders how I can just sit quietly and knit, no music, no tv, no talking, just knitting. People who knit understand that knitting is a form of meditation, a repetitive act which focuses the mind so that it can rest.

Though I learned how to knit when I was a young girl and I have made some fairly complicated sweaters along the way, I am only just becoming a real knitter. This is thanks to my friend Lisa who has taken me under her wing and lets me come to her house to work through my knitting difficulties and while I'm there we talk and sometimes, like today, I have a good cry. So knitting solo is a form of meditation and knitting with a friend is a form of therapy. How good is that?

April 10

Grief and Joy

This day is a significant anniversary for me, twenty-four years in recovery. In celebrating with the people who have helped me along this road, I talked in the meeting I led about holding grief and joy simultaneously. I have known this duality before in my life, but never with the intensity or depth that I know it now. I am coming to understand that grief will be with me forever, that there will always be a gaping hole in my life where Maggie is supposed to be, but also I know that side by side I must also allow myself to feel everything else that makes life full and rich, including joy.

My friend Diane sent me a column she had written in which she said, "The gift from that Easter service many years ago was the reminder that we are, by religion or culture, a people who believe in possibility. When our hearts are shattered we are sometimes shocked to discover that there is joy as well as pain inside. Out of the ashes of our mistakes, from our defeats and even our despair, we rise again in better lives."

The thought that I might not just survive Maggie's death, that I might actually be better for it is just coming into my consciousness. I feel how I am more present, better connected to people and the spirit, more appreciative, in less of a hurry, more open to be of service, better able to love. That all sounds so schmaltzy, but it's true.

April 11

Karl's Daughter

I needed a massage, badly. This was a new place, a new masseur. I had to fill out a form detailing any physical problems. Then, rather than giving the form the usual cursory review, this new guy, Karl, was really going into stuff and making suggestions of ways to work with different physical difficulties. I was sort of open and, at the same time, sort of thinking, *Okay, so when are we getting to my massage?*

Before we started, Karl asked about my goals for the session, and I said, "Overall relaxation, attention to this hip and shoulder that are bothering me, and I'm in mourning, so anything you can do to help move that along would be good." He asked, "Do you mind me asking about the mourning?" "No," I said, "my daughter died in November, suddenly, so I'm trying to learn to live positively and happily with grief." Our eyes met. "I know about that," Karl said softly, "my daughter died four years and two days ago."

Suddenly this healing encounter had taken on a very different dimension. We were moving into the massage as two parents who knew what it felt like to lose a child. Karl is a skilled masseur, with strong hands and a healing touch, but he also created a safe space for the grief and helped me to release some of it. During the two hours we spent together, Karl told me that his daughter died suddenly, at the age of twenty-one, from a malfunction in her brain. She was sleeping at her mother's home, and her mother found her. The parallels were extraordinary. Our encounter was a gift, certainly to me, perhaps to Karl as well.

April 12

Easter

Easter was never an important holiday in our Unitarian Universalist family, except in its pagan roots. We loved dying and hiding eggs, bringing newly blooming daffodils inside, eating chocolate bunnies and jelly beans. Stephen remembers Maggie bashing her head on the corner of the dining room table during an egg hunt, but I have forgotten that. Perhaps an older brother delights in such injuries and a mother blocks them out.

This Easter I was with my dear friend Phebe and her daughter Nora, both of whom loved Maggie. So, we had lots of stories and some tears. And it was interesting how in the wake of that, I was conscious of creating a loving, sweet time together, the stuff that future stories and tears might be made of. After Phebe and Nora returned from church, we worked outside in the garden, planting an herb bed, moving rocks and settling them into the dirt. The air and breeze were cool, but the sun was strong. We ate a luscious salad for lunch, and then I devoured a solid chocolate bunny, ears first.

April 13

Reporting

My friend Gregor Gibson, whose son was murdered in 1992, is a successful writer. It is what he always wanted to be, but to support his family, he became a book dealer, specializing in antiquarian maritime materials. After the murder, Gregor undertook a journey to discover how and why Wayne Lo set out to kill with an automatic weapon on that December night at Simon's Rock College. His investigation led him to write a book about the process: *Gone Boy*.

Since that book was well received and he had enjoyed the process of writing it, Gregor has continued to write and publish two more books, each to acclaim, while still maintaining his book business. I have just visited Gregor's website about his latest book, *Hubert's Freaks*. On the site, Gregor talks about the process of writing *Gone Boy* and how the act turned him from a victim to a reporter, that along the way, there was a profound shift from being someone who was suffering a wrenching loss to someone who was reporting on the circumstances that collided that night, and that he found himself empowered by being able to do something in response to Galen's death.

I understand exactly what he is talking about. This

collection of daily entries does the same for me. As I am experiencing some part of the grieving, there is another part of me that is watching the experience, trying to notice it as faithfully as possible. Interestingly, it doesn't feel like I create distance as a result of this detachment and objectivity, I think almost the opposite happens: I can go into the experience with more intensity and abandon because I know I am going to be okay.

April 14

Returning for Jeremy

Since Maggie's death, I have not wanted to return to Gilman, the school where I taught for fifteen years and from which I retired last June. I have felt too raw.

However, a few weeks ago, one of my former advisees invited me to attend the assembly in which the new recipients were to be inducted into the *Cum Laude* Honor Society. I wanted to be there for Jeremy, a student I greatly admire and feel genuinely fond of, so I went. I felt so strange, opening the door to the auditorium as I had done for fifteen years, almost every day, to attend assembly. It was this small, automatic, physical gesture, and the weight of the door, the shift of the light, maybe even a certain smell, that made me feel strangely suspended between being an outsider and being an intimate insider.

Both before and after the assembly, and then later at the reception, so many people greeted me with warmth. There was very little mention of Maggie's death, but the unspoken message that I was loved and supported and that many people had been thinking about me and sending me prayers was palpable. It wasn't difficult; I felt buoyed and glad that I had broken through the resistance to returning.

April 15

Cycles

I am ready to sew the seams of the sweater I've been making. I have two good books I consult for instruction on this sort of thing. One was given to me long ago by my grandmother, also Margaret. It is the *Readers Digest Complete Guide to Needlework* and is sort of like the *Joy of Cooking* (which she also gave me) in that it tells you how to do everything. The other book, a recent gift from Maggie, is entitled *stitch'n bitch, The Knitter's Handbook*, and it pretty much has the same information but in much hipper terms. That book is dedicated to the author's maternal grandmother who, like mine, died at the age of 104. I didn't really think about it as I consulted these two books, checking my alternatives for different seams with different stitches. It wasn't until I was sitting quietly and sewing, the rain streaming down the window, that I realized I had held in my hands legacies of these two women whom I've loved so dearly, neither of whom cared a whit for needlework, but both of whom cared enough about me to keep me in a good reference book.

April 16

Bereft Enough?

Now that Bill and I have been to four meetings of Bereaved Parents, I am feeling more comfortable and connected but no less affected by the shared pain. It is always hard for me the day afterwards, carrying not only my own emptiness and heartache but that of others I am coming to care about. This time though I am carrying this feeling of inadequacy because I don't seem to be as bereft as other parents. I know I loved Maggie with a very big heart. I know we had a sweet relationship that was more than mother/daughter, that was also friends and confidantes. I know we had really good times together, both simple times and special times. And I know my heart aches and that I have terrible pain at the loss of her presence, BUT, I am not bereft. I can laugh, I feel happiness and joy, I am carried by a powerful sense of her presence taking care of me and loving me. I sleep well; I am not depressed. On the one hand, I am grateful that each day comes and I am not crippled by grief, and on the other hand, I wonder what is wrong with me. Am I terribly shut down? Do I have a hard heart? Am I in denial? Is this part of the shock that in order to take care of myself I still can not feel the full loss of my daughter?

Others in the group say that the second year is harder. I can't think that way. I have to stay in this day. Comparing where I am to where I was or where I might be in a year seems like a fruitless and even dangerous occupation.

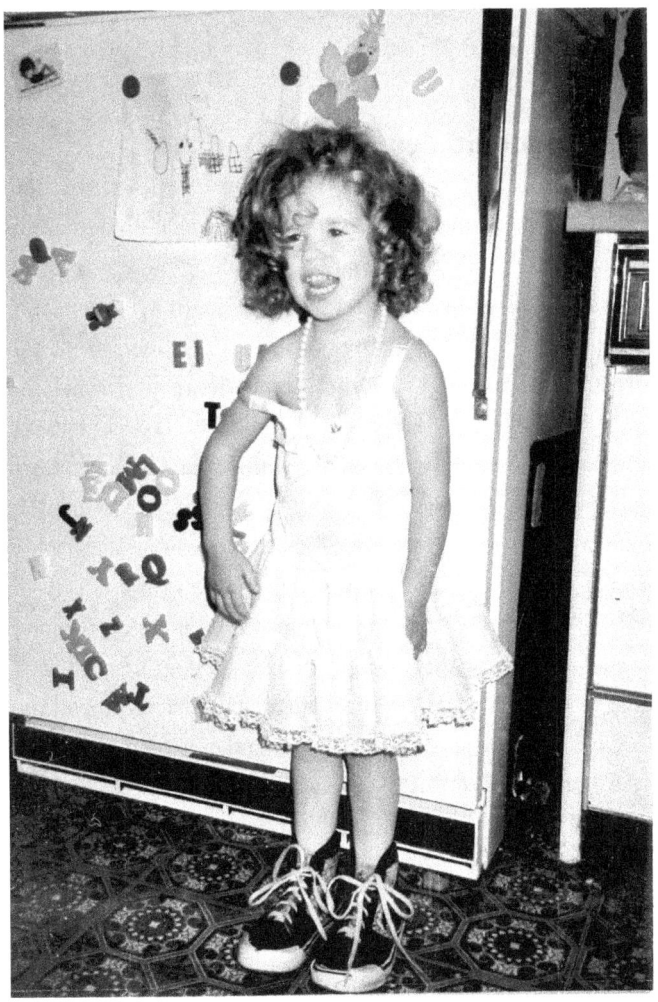

April 17

Girl in the Street

Jim and I were driving home from lunch with friends, top down on this beautiful spring day, breezing up our street, almost home, dodging the parked cars along the way, passing a group of kids, out of high school early? (maybe seniors?), a pack of them laughing and strolling along the side of the street. Suddenly, right in front of me, a girl peeled off the pack and rushed to the middle of the street, crouched down and picked something up, a flower I think, and I braked hard and slammed the horn. She leapt up, screaming, completely unaware that a car was there, and then swung back to her friends, falling into their arms, laughing and scared, all of them. My heart was beating wildly and I felt angry, so angry at her and them, that they were alive and so careless, and angry at myself that I almost hit her, that I am alive and so careless, that all of us are alive and not paying enough attention. I called out, "That was so close." "I know," she said, "I'm sorry." And then I thought, *But she was paying attention: to her friends, the warm sun, the freedom from school, and the flower in the street. She was in her moment, it just wasn't my moment.*

April 18

Epilepsy in the News

Since Maggie's death, epilepsy has been in the news. Senator Edward Kennedy had a seizure. John Travolta's son died of a seizure. President Obama's senior advisor, David Axelrod's daughter, Lauren, has epilepsy; his wife Susan is a founding board member and president of CURE, Citizens United for Research in Epilepsy. Their story was the feature in Parade magazine. The April 20, 2009, issue of *Newsweek* features a cover story on epilepsy, with an editorial by Jon Meacham, prompted by the one year anniversary of the death of Henry Foster Lapham, the four-year old son of his best friends; Henry died of SUDEP.

After Maggie died, everyone said, "We had no idea." Even some medical doctors and nurses within our circle of friends were shocked. Now it seems like everyone is talking about epilepsy and seizure disorders and the toll they can take on individuals and the people who love them. There is even a new website called TalkAboutIt.org, which was created by Greg Grunberg, star of NBC's HEROES and the father of a child with epilepsy, in collaboration with the Epilepsy Foundation. This is good publicity. We need public awareness, we need outcry, we need money, we need medical research, not just research to find good medications, for which people pay, but research to find a cure.

Maggie never made a fuss about her epilepsy. She wanted to live as normally as possible. For all the energy she put into causes, epilepsy was never one of them. That fight is up to us, the ones who loved her, who are left behind. And so we have added that to the mission for the Maggie Feiss Fund: help for people with epilepsy.

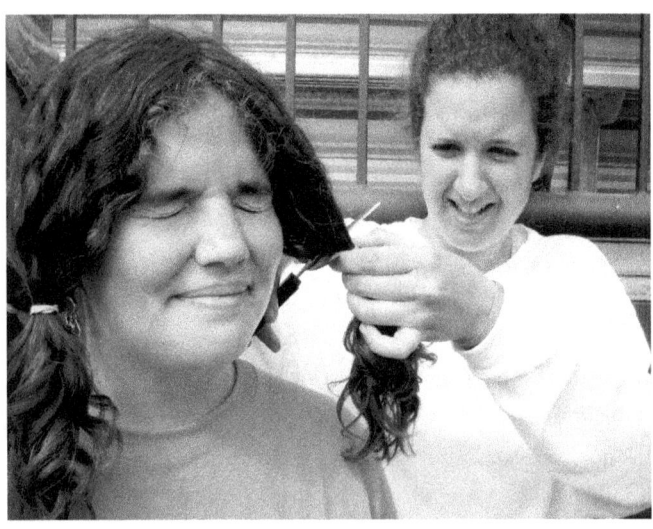

April 19

Door Jamb

Jim and I passed in the doorway to the kitchen and stopped to hug each other, as we often do. With my head pressed against his shoulder, I saw the door jamb with the markings of his boys' heights as they grew up, his boys who are now so tall and so far away in the world, but still alive. I reached my hand out and touched it and said, "Your boys." I hadn't known I needed to cry, but the tears rushed up, the moaning sobs from deep inside, and he held me, and he understood. I was crying for Maggie, for raising a child through all those marks on the door only to have her die. I was crying for gratitude that I now have his two boys in my life to be my children too. And perhaps these also were tears of any parent just missing those days when the children were little; that loss we all share. Though most of the time we are very happy to be through the grueling labor of active child rearing, there is sometimes that nostalgia for the past.

April 20

One More Visit

On April 9, Nick Adenhart, a 22 year-old rookie pitcher with the Los Angeles Angels, pitched six scoreless innings against Oakland, his first major league game. Afterwards, Nick told his father that he was leaving the hotel, where they were both staying, to go out for a few hours with some friends. On their way to a nightclub, a minivan, driven by Andrew Thomas Gallo, also 22, ran a red light and killed Adenhart and his two friends. Gallo has been charged with thee counts of murder, leaving an accident, and drunk driving.

Now when I read about tragic accidents like this, I think about the parents of all four of those boys, for whom, in an instant, everything changed, forever. I think about them getting the news, the disbelief and shock, and the aftermath, trying to put together a life.

At a memorial service for Adenhart, his high school catcher spoke, expressing the wish of everyone who loses someone they love suddenly, "If I could take one more visit to the mound . . ." I am touched by the longing of this catcher to cross that divide between the batter's box and the pitching mound for one last visit. Everything feels so precious.

April 21

Flirting With Death

This entry is hard to write. I have been avoiding it. It is another one in which I have to confess to feelings I am ashamed of. Part of me does not want to live. For all the glory I can find in life, there is this other side that feels ready to die. I am not going to take my life, but I'm not fighting for it either. I have not done a breast exam since Maggie died. When Jim, Mom, and I flew out west and the plane was pitching and creaking in terrible winds at landing, I felt sick, but not scared. I just thought, "I'm ready to die. Everything important to me is done." As soon as I write this, I want to qualify it: I do love and care about Stephen and Jim and my Mom and my brothers and Bill and my friends. I want to say: please don't overreact to this, please know that I am okay and this feeling is normal. It's just that death marks the edge of the space between Maggie's spirit and mine, and when it's my time, I will be ready to leap that chasm in a heartbeat.

April 22

The Maggie Card

A group that I am very involved in is in the middle of a controversial decision. When we met to discuss and vote, I made a strong case for one side and put forward a proposal. The proposal carried, quite strongly. Now, some of the people who disagreed with the decision are angry and hurt. One of them said to me this morning, "Many people who voted with you were casting sympathy votes." I just stared at him in disbelief. I don't believe that that is true and even if it were, what kind of person says something like that?

April 23

Garden

All my adult life I have loved tending a garden. Pulling weeds, preparing soil, planting, harvesting, all are good therapies and also often carry meaning alongside the immediate task. All the metaphors of gardening have taken up space in my mind at one time or another.

I have never been happier for spring than I am this year, never more ready to clear the dead leaves from the beds and to see that my perennials and herbs have survived the winter, never more eager to begin planting my vegetable garden.

April 24

Without Tears

Jim and I went to a fundraiser at the library and ran into an old friend of Jim's whom I have not seen since Maggie died. I knew that she had lost her son a long time ago. We talked about how there is a bond and a comfort between people who have been through this, who understand. She said, "Some day, you will be able to talk about Maggie's death without tears."

April 25

Shoe Shrine

I am reading Jennifer Martin's *Star Child*. The book is much like what I have undertaken here, short reflections about the progress of mourning her 23 year old son's death. The writing is poignant, mirroring many feelings that I am having. Tonight I read of Martin's experience with her son Kelly's shoes. She concludes that section saying, "We will always wish that our children would need their shoes" (65).

At Bill's house, just inside the front door, under a chest of drawers, is a pile of Maggie's shoes. Both our kids were famous for having loads of shoes and leaving them all over the house, but Maggie was the worst. Bill collected those shoes from around his house the night of Maggie's death and there they stay, right by the door, waiting for her to come home.

April 26

Apology

Jim and his sister own a Christmas tree farm, and since Maggie's death, I have taken great solace in going to the farm and working. Outdoor, manual labor is good for me; I have always loved getting my hands dirty, working hard, being able to see the results of my efforts, and being in the fresh air and sunshine. I even love getting hot and sweaty. I always find such work very therapeutic; I can lose myself in it.

I like to take my music and headphones and sing while I drive the tractor or mow or haul and stack wood. I sing heartily, and no one hears me except the rabbits and deer, field mice and hawks, ground hogs and butterflies. I revel in my voice flowing into the green of the grass and trees and the blue of the sky.

Often, I cry. I might sense the tears working their way up or they might break out suddenly, but they come, and I get to something I may not have realized before. Today it was Grace Potter's song "Apologies" that broke me open. There I was, driving the tractor, singing, and bawling my eyes out as Gracie belted, "Oh he said it's crazy / How love stays with me / You know it hurts me / Cause I don't wanna fight this war / It's amazing to see me reading through this scene / Of love and fear and apologies." And I realized that the aftermath of Maggie's death has been a war, a constant fight for equilibrium and peace and sanity, and I don't want to fight any more. I'm tired and I don't have the heart for it. I know the answer lies in surrender, in letting my higher power and other people take care of me, in not having to be so strong.

And then I thought about apologies and wondered through my tears whether there was anything I felt I wanted to tell Maggie I was sorry for, any amends I needed to make, and the answer was right there, very clear: *I am sorry for the pain that came with the dissolution of our family. We all were torn apart, but none of us so harshly as you. I always felt badly that we hurt you so deeply, but now I am especially sad that in your short life, you had to bear that sorrow.*

One thing that makes this better is that Bill and I are loving and supporting each other well these days. Maggie always wanted us to get back together; maybe now that her spirit is boundless, she is enabling us to do that in a way that we can.

April 27

Babysitters

This morning I picked up *When Things Fall Apart*, by Pema Chodron and was astonished to turn, almost haphazardly, to a section that flips on its head what I often feel about my higher power and the ways it embodies itself in Maggie. Chodron, a Buddhist, reminds us of the first noble truth: suffering happens. The source of peace and freedom is not in giving our lives over to a higher power which will take care of us, a "babysitter," but rather in "relaxing with the ambiguity and uncertainty of the present moment without reaching for anything to protect ourselves" (48).

I suspect that this is one of those dangerous dualities that humans are so quick to formulate. I am suspicious of anything that invites my brain to think it can handle life without surrender to something greater than it, and I am simultaneously open to the idea that all religious/spiritual formulations are distractions from the incomprehensible divine. That said, and all theory aside, to embody God in my daughter brings me some peace, because it makes both that power and my daughter more present. Maggie always was a great babysitter, much in demand, because she loved to play.

Meg Tipper

April 28

Moon Smile

I was out for an evening walk, a beautiful, warm, spring night, light still waning at 8:30, but I was not noticing. My head was full of chatter, nothing as lofty as missing Maggie, just noise. Suddenly, I was hit by the most amazing smell; it stopped me cold. Beside me was a lilac bush, loaded with blossoms, heavy with perfume. I just stood there and breathed and suddenly felt full of the rush of being in my body. This same person who, one second before, was missing it all was transformed in an instant: alive! As I began to walk again, I was aware of the sky, the lattice of tree branches, budding, and then, revealed by the clouds pushed aside by the wind, the underside sliver of a moon, a smile. "Thanks, Mags," I said out loud, "I love you."

April 29

"I Hate Mother's Day"

Today, at the start of a twelve-step meeting, I overheard a woman complaining, "I hate mother's day!" She said she always has expectations that her husband and child will deliver gifts or meals and then what they come up with never fulfill her hopes. She said, "I told them this year I will just get gourmet-to-go and all they have to do is heat it up."

I turned my head and prayed really hard not to be judgmental. Then, after the meeting, she came to me and hugged me and said, "I noticed you during the meeting and I thought about you and Maggie and what I said about mother's day and I am so sorry."

April 30

High School Play

John Rowell, one of my good friends from Gilman, is the director of the annual spring musical, always a great show and quite the extravaganza. I heard that one of my old advisees had a lead this year, and I was eager to go to opening night to support those special people and others whom I knew were involved. Jim and I met another teacher from the school for a bite to eat and then we sat together for the show. I had been so focused on seeing the show and my friends that I had not thought at all about how hard it would be to sit in the audience in the same theatre in which I had watched Maggie perform for each of her years in middle and high school.

Maggie was not a great actress, nor did she have an especially striking voice. She could dance, but she was not a dancer. What Maggie did have, which made her a joy to watch, was a passion for acting. She so loved being on stage, so enjoyed everything about performing, was so relaxed and happy in the process of entertaining, that she was radiant. People always said that no matter what her part, she stole the show, because you really couldn't take your eyes off her.

Standing at the Edge

May 1

Gorilla

Our neighborhood yard sale is tomorrow and I have been getting everything ready. I had been pretty systematic in packing up my apartment, but some boxes of Maggie's had been packed up after she finished high school. I opened one box and found old notebooks and journals, pocketbooks, videos, and books. On top of the box was an enormous stuffed gorilla Bill's mother had given her. I cracked up.

I remembered Maggie in her cameo as a gorilla in *Cabaret!* her senior year. She loved her stint in the gorilla suit. In the box, I also found some memorabilia from Bryn Mawr, her high school, including an embroidered sash, which each girl wears in the annual spring tradition known as "gym drill." Tomorrow Maggie's class will gather for their 5th year reunion, which will include participation in this gym drill event. So, all in all, I figured that Maggie had delivered me a gift today: an opportunity to make everyone laugh. I have pinned the sash around the gorilla and will bring it to the event. That way, her friends can carry her with them as they march down the field. Maggie wasn't going to miss this.

May 2

Six Months

It was a big Maggie day. At the yard sale, I was really happy as her possessions found new homes with people who wanted or needed them: her calculator to a mother and son who had just been talking about how he needed one to prepare for his PSATs, her Max stuffed toy to a little boy named Justin whose favorite book was *Where the Wild Things Are*, her *Friends* DVD to two women in their 60s who were out for a girls' yard sale spree on the Saturday morning.

Later, at Maggie's high school, I met up with Mom, Bill, Stephen, and many of Bill's family members to receive the Young Alumnae Award for Maggie. I shared an album with her classmates who had gathered for their fifth reunion: high school photos and memorabilia. There were hugs, tears, and, among her friends, that disbelief that can accompany thoughts of Maggie's death.

At the formal award ceremony, I was surprised and delighted that the recipient just before Maggie was Mary Shoemaker, hands down Maggie's favorite teacher at the school. Maggie and Mary were kindred free spirits, and they loved each other. In Mary's note to me after Maggie died, she said, "I usually think I'm pretty good at making words say what I want them to, but I find myself completely unable to express to you my sense of grief and loss that I will never see your wonderful, ebullient girl again. Without her wild curls, her joyous and ready laugh, her generous affection, the world is a colder place. I simply cannot tell you how completely you, and she, are in my thoughts." That Mary and Maggie should receive the same award on the same day is fitting, but the connection goes even more eerily deep.

I brought the gorilla in its yellow and white sash and it was the perfect embodiment of Maggie's presence. Her classmates hugged it, posed for photos with it, carried it snuggled among them, and then finally held it aloft as they finished their march in the traditional walk down the field. The gorilla and Maggie made us all smile. And now for the really amazing part: in the scene in Cabaret in which Maggie performed the duet as the gorilla—the boy playing the part opposite her was Mary's son, Tom.

Some may believe in coincidence if they want to, but for me, this is another example of the magic a spirit can work who still wants to make its presence felt in this world.

May 3

Exhausted

After a day of preparation and then a day of "up," I was totally exhausted. Jim and I slept late and were so happy to awaken to the sound of rain, an invitation to laziness. We did get together with Stephen, Bill, and Terry for crabs at Nick's. The last time I was there was in the late summer when Jim, Maggie, and I took Meghan, a friend new to Baltimore, there for her first crab feast. Maggie had reveled in teaching Meghan how to pick crabs and showing her just how happily dirty one gets.

I spent the rest of the afternoon uploading some photos onto Facebook and doing some yoga and meditation. Then Jim and I watched a movie and crashed. I often tell people that I do not accomplish much in a day, and, compared to my teaching life, that is true of most days, but this day, in the aftermath of a demanding emotional event, I was even more wasted than normal, and that's okay.

Meg Tipper

May 4

She Made Us Cry

My brother Bill told me several weeks ago that Maggie had communicated to him in his meditation that she wanted me to see a medium. Having just dropped considerable money to consult the psychic, this seemed like a lot to ask, but being the sucker I am for making my daughter happy, even after her death, I contacted Janet and set up an appointment.

I realized that I was nervous as I drove there. I talked to Maggie, my grandmother, my father, my ex-father-in-law, even a few friends who have died, telling them all what I was doing and asking that they use this opportunity if there was anything they needed me to know.

Janet is a pretty, gentle, white-haired, ex-pat English woman. We sat in her office with her dog, and she explained that in contrast to a psychic who tunes into the client's energy, she receives from the realm of spirits of those who have died.

The experience was deeply emotional, tapping into our yearning to reach across this separation caused by the death of people we love. I began to cry shortly after she began, and Janet pushed the box of tissues towards me saying, "This is what they will put on my grave: She made us cry."

I can't say with certainty that I believe Janet has the gift of communicating with spirits, but I can affirm that our session was therapeutic and consoling. She certainly read me and the sorts of things that I needed to hear. I am coming to see all of what I am doing as a constellation of resources, each with different pathways into the complex and vast physical, emotional, mental, and spiritual landscape of grieving.

May 5

Gutted

It is another gray, damp, cold day and I still feel gutted. I have been doing things that are good for me: sleeping plenty, eating well, praying, but I still have this constant emptiness and listlessness. It's all I can do to write these few sentences.

Someone in recovery asked me for help today and I waffled. Now I feel guilty, because so many people have carried me for the last six months, and I am sure that it would make me feel better to be of service. But at that moment, I felt like I had no energy, nothing to give, that I would be selling her short. I did give her my phone number, but did not offer to be her sponsor, which was what she was asking for. I'm trying not to beat myself up for this. I am trying to acknowledge that God was probably giving me exactly what I needed, a chance to think about someone else, and that when I am given another chance to help, I can move towards it rather than feeling empty and afraid.

May 6

No Important Decisions

Jim and I have been talking about a financial investment which would be quite significant for my cash flow. It would yield a handsome return after a few years but would mean a much greater degree of financial dependence on him for the short term. I was talking to Helen about it and she said, wisely, "It is important to remember that you are not thinking very clearly right now; it would probably be wise not to make any major decisions." This advice rang true; it is advice I would give to someone in my position.

When people are new in twelve-step recovery programs, they are advised not to make any major changes in their lives for the first year. Then, after they are completely detoxed and much more aware of who they are, without the influence of chemicals, they are in a better position to make thoughtful and healthy decisions about their lives. I imagine the period following a sudden death is much the same: there is a new me emerging, and until I know who I am, it is better not to go too far along in thinking I know what I want or how my life should be.

May 7

Love

In a meeting, I shared about how flat I have been feeling, how I am scared that the wind is gone from my sails, how overpowered I am sometimes by the depth of this loss and the prospect of this pain. Then the basket was passed around for contributions, and I put in a five-dollar bill and took out my change. As I smoothed the ones to put away in my wallet, I saw that printed neatly across the end of one bill was the word LOVE. And I knew I could make it through another day.

May 8

Artichokes

Maggie loved artichokes. We thought it was a strange food for a child to adore, but then we realized that she liked artichokes less for their taste than for their fun. Peeling off the leaves with our fingers, scraping the meat off with our teeth and savoring the process slowed everyone down to Maggie's speed of eating and made the meal a party. Later she would discover the same pleasure in picking crabs.

Last night Jim and I had artichokes for dinner, and I tried to muster the pleasure I knew Maggie would want me to feel in eating them, but, honestly, mine tasted slightly bitter, and the heart was heavy.

May 9

Sea Turtle

Jim and I have joined Kendal and Janet in Cozumel, Mexico, for some relaxation, sun, and scuba diving. The last time we were supposed to go diving was five days after Maggie died, and, of course, we cancelled the trip. I remember thinking then that diving would be good for me, that I could escape into my water world with just my breath and the fish and coral and sponges and maybe forget everything for a few moments.

Getting back under the water is always a thrill for me, and it brings so much peace. The first time I experienced the sensation of breathing, and hovering, neutral buoyancy, under water, I thought, "Why did we ever come out?" Our first dive in Cozumel was no exception, and in addition to the magic of the sea and the fish, I got to fly on the current in a drift dive. We had seen many beautiful fish on that first wall dive, including a huge Grouper and a big, green Moray eel swimming together.

Our safety stop parked us conveniently over a shallow section of reef so that we could enjoy more underwater sightseeing while we prepared our bodies for the final ascent to the surface. Just after everyone else headed up and I was about to follow, a sea turtle about the size of a large cantaloupe swam right up to me. I was delighted, and simply watched as she swam slowly and gracefully near, tipping her back towards me so that I could see her beautiful markings. As she turned to swim away, she was backlit by the sun through the water, languid strokes of her short legs propelling her into the light. It was a sweet mother's day gift.

May 10

"She Has Me!"

Our dive master, Norman, told us that his mother was visiting him from another part of Mexico for a weekend on Cozumel. We asked what he had planned for her for mother's day and he shrugged, "Nothing, really, she has me!" I joined in as everyone, even the men, gave Norman a hard time about neglecting his mother and thinking so highly of himself, but underneath my gentle teasing, I felt heartsick. Having my child was certainly all I wanted for my mother's day gift.

May 11

Tiptoeing

I lay awake on our hard Mexican bed, listening to the sharp cries of birds and watching the first light catch the stucco sides of buildings and illuminate the sky into a glowing blue. Sure that I was not going to go back to sleep, I let my mind grab onto thoughts and then, feeling peaceful and safe with Jim breathing deeply beside me, I allowed myself to go towards thinking of Maggie. Usually thoughts of her come to me and I have to create some protection against them, but this was my step, to tiptoe towards nurturing my memories.

I chose her first bedroom, the one to which we brought her home after she was born. I remembered turning the space from my little office into her baby bedroom, recalled where we placed the furniture and how I had decorated, heard her cries as she revved up, needing to be fed, and later how she would talk to her animals and then throw them all out of her crib when she was ready to get up, liberating them as she wished to be.

I couldn't stay long, but it was a start.

May 12

Chair Rock, Heart Rock

I had become chilled during my second dive of the day and once back to land, couldn't wait to stretch out on one of the lounge chairs at the dive shop and soak in the sun. I lay, warming, listening to the waves sloshing against the concrete sea wall. Perhaps it was something softening in me as I let go of the feeling of being cold, but quite suddenly I began to cry, tears spilling from behind my closed eyes. I wasn't sobbing, there was no movement of my body, so I was surprised to feel my chair rock; I thought Jim must have come up behind me. I sat up and looked, but no one was there. Strange. *Okay*, I thought, *I've warmed up now, I'd better go help put away the gear.* As I began to walk back to the deck, I glanced down to where the sea wall met the beach, a flat bit of cement and large, flat rocks. In one of the rocks was an indentation, clearly in the shape of a heart. Maggie keeps reminding me to feel the love.

May 14

Friends

On television almost constantly here in Mexico are reruns of episodes of *Friends*. Maggie went through a huge *Friends* stage in middle school and early high school. I'm sure she saw every show at least once. She and her best friend at the time, Emily, would do all night *Friends* marathons. So, as Janet and Kendal and I watched Phebe try to teach Joey French, and Monica and Chandler worry that their adopted baby would grow up to be an axe murderer, and Ross try to convince Rachel not to fly to Paris, Maggie was never far away.

May 15

"Since Maggie's Death"

I was talking to Kendal, and, as so often happens, our conversation turned to our mother and how she is doing (great, especially as compared to her contemporaries). Kendal said, "Since Maggie's death, it seems like Mom isn't letting the little things get to her so much." I think that's true, but what struck me in that moment was the words: "Maggie's death." I think about that event, that fact, that idea, and all its permutations so often, and I write those words here and speak them to friends and family over and over again, but I can probably count on one hand the number of times they have been spoken to me. Perhaps people refrain from saying them as a way to protect me. I don't know. I do know that I appreciated Kendal's speaking of Maggie's death as a marker event--the words giving it some weight in someone else's world.

May 16

"Cultivating Gratitude"

I picked up the Winter, 2009, newsletter at the Bereaved Parents meeting and have saved it because of an article by Abigale Fuller entitled "Cultivating Gratitude." I know about the power of gratitude; I have long practiced making gratitude lists as a way to shift my thinking. But this article affirmed gratitude as a way to process grieving. How can that be? I do not have a grateful bone in my body for Maggie's death. But I do for her life. Intentionally remembering, celebrating, honoring, and cherishing that life makes me happy, and grateful. And, as Fuller points out, as a way to help the healing from this loss, I can remember and cultivate gratitude for my own life too.

May 17

Family Dinners

My brothers, Kendal and Charlie, have been in Baltimore for a family meeting. Twice we got together for dinner: my Mom and her four children and Jim. I have been reflecting on how differently I feel about my place in the family now. I knew, growing up, that my brothers resented me. I was the oldest child and the only girl and therefore different and privileged. They were a tribe of three boys, and they played together, plotted against me, and teased me terribly. We fought all the time. As we got older, I felt that my brothers loved me, but didn't like me very much, thought I was too serious and stuffy. Then I had my first child ten years before any one of them did and our priorities were different. Finally, there was recovery, which meant another different path for me.

However, as we have aged, we have drawn closer. We began to gather every summer with our children at Lake Paupac, the Quaker community in the Pocono Mountains where we went in the summers as children. Those leisurely days at the lake with each other, our Mom and our extended families have woven the strands of the family much tighter. Within the last decade we have lost our grandmother and two of the four of us have gone through separations and divorces, we have come to know how much we need each other.

And now Maggie is dead, that firecracker of a girl who lit us all up. I feel my brothers, my Mom, and I drawing even closer around the pain and loss, finding no small solace in being together.

May 18

A Brood

My youngest brother and three of my cousins will celebrate their 50th birthdays this year. Thinking of them recently made me remember all the summer vacations we had together, my mother's family. Mom had three siblings, and between the four children, my grandparents had thirteen grandchildren. We were a large brood.

I already knew that my two children would not produce thirteen grandchildren. However, I always imagined that there would be plenty of grandchildren to spoil, plenty of cousins to form their own little brood. Maggie and Stephen were so close that I knew they would be sure their children were too.

Now Stephen's children will have no first cousins on his side. I know it doesn't make any sense to mourn this loss, something I didn't have and might never have had. But I did have the idea, the image, the dream, and it is hard to let it go.

May 19

Tigger Mug & Frother

Maggie gave me a Disney mug for my birthday, at least ten years ago. It's green with bright yellow flowers and one Tigger on each side, a huge smile on his face, his "arms" lifted up in delight. I love having my morning coffee in this mug.

When I was in Florida at Christmas time, Janet treated me to coffee with frothed milk. I was so pleased with the luxury of it that she helped me find my own frother on overstock.com. Now I not only have my Tigger mug, I heat my milk in the microwave, froth it up, and pour it onto the top of my coffee. It makes for a really decadent morning treat. Sometimes it makes me forget the sadness.

May 20

"God, I Miss Maggie."

My aunt, Maggie's godmother called me today, as she has many times, just to check in. She left me a message telling me she loves me, relating something about Maggie that she was remembering which had made her smile, and closing with, "God, I miss Maggie." Such a message is deeply comforting. Perhaps others might feel differently, but, for me, when people who love Maggie recall her and share their own grief at her loss, it somehow diminishes my pain.

May 21

"I Know You Won't Mind."

I had made some tentative plans to get together for lunch with someone whom I have not seen for quite awhile, but whom I have known well, worked with, and feel very fond of. In the process of organizing our get-together, she sent me an email: "I know you won't mind that I have invited some other friends." These are people who care about me, knew Maggie and gave to her memorial fund, two people whom I like and normally would enjoy spending time with, but all of a sudden, the lunch felt like too much for me. While I could handle one person, three was a party. Fortunately, I did not hesitate to say I couldn't do it, for which my friend was grateful. She and I will get together another time.

Long before Maggie died, I learned my limits with socializing. I have a low tolerance for parties, groups large enough for there to be more than one conversation going, and sometimes I don't have much patience for any conversation at all. These days, I have even less stamina than normal. And so I have to take people in small doses and not say yes to something I don't feel up to.

May 22

Sailing

This past summer at Paupac, Maggie asked me to teach her to sail. I was nervous because of her recent frequent seizures and insisted she wear a life jacket, which made her crazy, but we still had fun in our little Sunfish on our little mountain lake with the fluky wind. We tacked all over, rounding marks as though we were racing. We sailed into the beach, making a grand entrance as Maggie loved to do.

I have always loved to sail. The wind, bracing and powerful, pushing the boat. The physics of angles and weight and wind. The peace of slicing the water with a light grip on the tiller. Sun setting on a long run home. Today, Helen, who has been my climbing companion all winter, took me sailing. We left the Baltimore Inner Harbor and tacked out to the Key Bridge, a good long way, exchanging a light breeze in the protected waters of the harbor for a brisk wind and whitecaps by the time we reached the bridge and turned back. It was a beautiful, peaceful afternoon.

The sail with Helen reminded me of Maggie less because of those days of sailing last summer than another time we cruised the Baltimore harbor. Almost exactly a year ago, after Maggie came home, following her graduation from

USC, we threw her a party aboard a large boat called the Black Eyed Susan. It was an extravagance, but then Maggie somehow brought out everyone's extravagant side! We had a beautiful summer evening for a cruise, and the boat was a perfect venue for a gathering of the diverse ages and circles of Maggie's many friends. Nate, in from California, coordinated the music from his iPod and Maggie, of course, led the dancing. My favorite memory is of Maggie dancing with the young daughter of her neurologist. I remember at the time thinking, "My god, if this is what we're doing for her graduation, I hate to think what her wedding is going to look like!" Now I am so thankful that we pulled out all the stops when we did.

May 23

Greenmount Cemetery

I am wiped out following a morning tour of Greenmount Cemetery with Jim and my Mom. Wayne Schaumburg, our guide, is a natural teacher: knowledgeable, funny, and great at pacing. We saw the graves of many of Baltimore's leaders of the 19th century. This beautiful old cemetery was created on the grounds of the home of my great, great, great grandfather, Robert Oliver, a wealthy Baltimore merchant.

We got a shout out as the celebrated ancestors on the tour. Jim took a picture of Mom and me in front of the Oliver obilisk. We stopped to pay homage at the family plot. We admired the beautiful trees, the variety of sculptures. We learned that the Victorian graveyard was all about making a beautiful, bucolic environment in which the dead could "sleep" or "rest" and the living could take a walk or have a picnic and feel cushioned from the loss of death.

But, of course, death was everywhere. Both in the beginnings and endings and in the spaces or stones still to be filled in. The first person buried at the new cemetery was Olivia Whitridge, in December 1839. She was two years old. There were so many gravestones for children. The most moving was "Sleeping Children" commissioned by Hugh and Sara Sisson to commemorate the deaths of their five children. The renowned sculptor William Henry Rinehart carved two children, lying asleep in each others' arms, their heads on a pillow. This sweet sculpture rests on top of a vault on which is carved the names of Mary (who died in 1853), Sara, James, Kate, and William (who died in 1861). Hugh and Sara mourned the deaths of five children in eight years. The thought is staggering to me.

Finally we passed the crematorium, the one to which Maggie's body was sent.

May 24

The Bath

Almost every night since Maggie died, I have taken a bath. It is not really about getting clean. I pour in an excessive amount of bubble bath, run the water as hot as I can stand it, and fill the tub as high as it will go. It is shockingly wasteful. Then I tip toe into the water and ease my body down slowly. The water is just under my chin and the bubbles cluster around my neck and hair. I close my eyes and breathe and try to think of nothing. It is often my best meditation of the day, the closest I can come to peace.

There is irony here because Maggie went through a period in her early childhood when she was terrified of water. Baths were a terrible struggle--there was no distracting or consoling her. When it came down to the necessity of a hair wash, Bill or I had to take her into the shower with her clinging to our chest and crying desperately through the whole thing. Slowly this terror passed, but Maggie never loved water the way I do.

When I saw Anat, she told me that Maggie will be happy to have her ashes scattered anywhere we choose, except over the water.

May 25

Money Stuff

All my life I have been compulsive about paying bills and keeping close track of my money. While it has never been something I have enjoyed doing, I habitually have entered all my credit card charges, reconciled my accounts monthly, and been on top of what money is coming in and what is going out.

Since Maggie died, I have been very lax, almost to the point of irresponsible about these things. To date I have not forgotten to pay a bill, but I have come close. It is dreadfully hard to summon the energy for my financial life. I have piles of papers on my desk and no idea whether anything in there is really important.

I have been hoping that as time passes, this difficulty will lift, but it feels like it is getting worse. I think it might be a sign of depression. On the other hand, maybe Maggie's death is just lightening me up a little, after all, I have been kind of hyper responsible.

May 26

Yoga

I have started a new yoga class and I love being in a class again. While I have had my own practice off and on since 1975, doing yoga with other people and working with a teacher always takes me to a deeper level. In my first class with Leslie, she brought us up from a forward bend by breathing into the spine and lifting, slowly and mindfully. It was a very intense opening, and as my shoulders rounded back and my neck curved up and my head came to rest on the top of my spine, I felt exhilarated. Then we stood in Tadasana, mountain pose, very solid, eyes closed, and focused on the fifth chakra, Vissudha, at the base of the throat which is connected to expression and faith. Very suddenly, I began to cry, not a tightening of the throat cry, but just freely flowing tears. I did not feel particularly sad; I felt open and moved. It was strange and really lovely.

May 27

Rehoboth Beach, DE

I tried to let Memorial Day weekend slide by without associations, and I was doing really well until today. This traditional start of summer was the time when Maggie and I would take a road trip in my convertible and head to the beach for sun, shopping, movies, pedicures, junk food and lots of girl talk. It was an annual ritual and a sort of bacchanalia of all the sorts of mother-daughter fun we had not gotten enough of over the course of the school year.

This past weekend, I concentrated on Jim, my Mom and on Jim's son, Ira and his girlfriend who were down from New York City. We had some good family time, and the days passed without my feeling too flat. However, today, Helen's daughter, Jess, who is just a year younger than Maggie, came climbing with us, and towards the end of our session, Jess and I were sitting on the floor of the gym, hunkered down for some straight talk about when and how she should break up with her boyfriend. I loved touching into her life like that, loved helping her think through the situation, loved her youth and sweetness.

If Maggie and I had been at Rehoboth Beach last weekend, we would have had that talk, or the how it is not a good time to have a boyfriend conversation, or the how to get a guy interested strategy session. There would have been guy talk, for sure. And, as much as I was loving talking with Jess, part of me wanted her to be Maggie.

May 28

No Emotional Resilience

I had two difficult conversations within an hour of each other. Nothing major, in one I had something difficult to say; in another I had to hear something that wasn't what I wanted to hear. I never have been comfortable with confrontation or discord, but I know how to hold my own and in the past, I have weathered those kinds of conversations without tremendous effort. Now, however, I feel depleted, I have no emotional resilience. I just want to go to bed, pull the covers over my head, and cry.

May 29

"Maggie's Online"

We have kept up Maggie's Facebook page since she died and many of her friends continue to write on it. It is a sweet memorial. I changed Maggie's "status" to say "Love . . .love . . .LOVE" and a few minutes later a chat came in from Sophie who told me that she saw Maggie's status change and thought, "oh good, Maggie's online." That made me cry to read it, knowing that there are other people who still struggle with believing that Maggie really is gone. Then came that cold flood in her gut, and Sophie went to Maggie's page to read what people have written lately. She said she had been all riled up with worry over her last exam tomorrow and reading Maggie's wall calmed her down.

May 30

Between Sleep and Awakening

Most often my first moments of the day involve some sort of coming to terms with the fact of Maggie's death, and, more often than not, this process is quick and startling and painful. However, this morning, something different happened. I felt Maggie inside me and, in my very barely awake consciousness, I considered the possibility that the fullness of this presence, the intimacy, constancy, and comfort of it, might be enough. I felt in some strange way that I am closer to Maggie now in her death than I would be able to be if she were still alive. To write this now makes it seem crazy, but in that moment, those feelings made sense, and I was grateful for them.

May 31

Space for Grieving

I talked with Stephen today. Now that his graduate classes have ended, his coaching is over, and school is winding down, he has more time for his feelings to catch up with him. I figured this might happen. He didn't exactly sound down, maybe more subdued. I asked whether it might be time to see Kathleen, the counselor Maggie and I met in the fall.

June 1

UCal

Stephen has two really close friends his age at work, Scott and UCal. Stephen and Scott have co-taught several classes and have led two summer school trips together. Stephen and UCal have coached the Varsity Boys Soccer team, have played pick up soccer for years, and get together for drinks after work every Friday. On Saturday afternoon, UCal was in the middle of playing a soccer game when he died suddenly of a heart complication. He was a Guidance Counselor at Newton North High School, beloved by the students, a fine young man, newly married. I think about his parents in Jamaica.

I am worried about my son. As he said, when he called me today with the news, "It's too much."

I also have felt fragile ever since he told me. I think, *It could have been Stephen.*

June 2

Words

People continue to ask me how I'm doing, which I appreciate. But then I have the problem of trying to put my feelings into words. I am past the point of being totally devastated, when simply looking into a friend's eyes and not saying anything sufficed. Now, some progress report seems to be in order, and so I recount the many pleasures in the traveling Jim and I have done and cite the ways in which I am taking care of myself and having fun. I express my gratitude for all the support and love I am still receiving. Sometimes I tell people how writing helps and retell something that I have recorded here or promise to send them an entry or two. But overall, I have two feelings, one is flat-out hypocrisy because while all of this is "true," none of it honestly gets at how I'm really doing, and the other feeling is betrayal, and this is more disturbing. How can I reduce the aftermath of Maggie's death to these markers of emotional well-being? Perhaps that is why the Bereaved Parents group is comforting, because everyone understands that while we seem to be people functioning in the world, one gaping part of us will always be a ghost, having traveled to the other side with our child.

June 3

Premonition of Death

Jim and I watched *Milk*, staring Sean Penn in an Oscar winning role as Harvey Milk, the first openly gay person elected to public office in this country. It is an excellent movie about an amazing man. Milk received death threats because of his sexuality and his political activism. In the movie, Milk dictates the significant moments from his life into a tape recorder, the explicit reason being the possibility that he might die. However, long before that, he says that he will not reach fifty, and then goes on to live the last eight years of his life with such passion and intensity. It made me think again about the possibility that Maggie foresaw that her life would be short. Even before she developed epilepsy, she was a ball of fire. I keep returning to the way she lived so fully, and then to the reconnections with people from her past that she made in the summer and fall before her death. Who knows if she felt something?

June 4

Name Tags

I finally have the energy and inclination to start a quilt project. It is not the quilt I will make from Maggie's clothes, nor the one I will make with photos and other memorials, I am not ready to tackle those. This quilt will be a wedding present for Stephanie and Chris; so I have until the end of October to finish. I bought the fabrics last summer when I went to New York City to see Robbie for a day and we spent a decadent few hours at The City Quilter (133 West 25th Street). I am excited.

In cleaning up the room I will use (quilting takes space) and organizing my sewing supplies, I came across a clear, zip-lock, plastic bag, with a strip of iron-on name tags: one after the other, in black block letters:

> MAGGIE FEISS
> MAGGIE FEISS
> MAGGIE FEISS

They had been there since June of 1998, when I was getting Maggie's clothes ready for her first sleep-away camp, where she had some fun and made some friends, but returned home with head lice, thereby souring the experience! I remember ironing the name tags onto T-shirts and shorts and finally giving Maggie a Sharpie with instructions to just write MOF on her socks and underwear. Going through Maggie's clothes after she died, I found things still marked with these tags and initials! That girl never got rid of anything.

So I am faced with the practical reality that Maggie will never need these name tags, but I don't have the heart to throw them away.

June 5

Interior Landscape

During shavasana, Leslie, my yoga instructor, suggested that we notice our interior landscape, and I immediately felt a clutch. This is a place I routinely fill my mind with trivia to avoid noticing. On examination, I found it to be barren, dry, stark and glaring, and almost lifeless. I immediately thought of Death Valley and how comfortable I felt there. I also thought about the contrast to the fecund excess of Baltimore right now, after a record spring rainfall, with the ground and air saturated, and everything looking like a jungle. It is too much lushness really and perhaps explains why I have been sleeping almost ten hours a night and still feeling tired.

June 6

Past Tense

A few weeks ago, after yoga class, several of us were talking about our butts, and I told my fellow students and Leslie, our instructor, about Maggie's glorious butt. The story I loved most was of her walking with a friend north on Broadway out of Fells Point in Baltimore. They heard the unmistakable thrump thrump of a bass coming up behind them. As a large SUV rolled slowly by, a darkly tinted window slid down, a handsome man's head craned around and then double-taked, a beat, before he said, "You shouldn't be white, girl!" Maggie loved telling that story. With her extravagant hair and butt, surely she was a *sista*. We laughed, loving our own butts a little more. On my walk home, I thought about telling that story in the past tense and how no one in that group of women but I knew that Maggie was no longer alive.

Yesterday after class, when just Leslie and I were talking, she asked about my children. "I know you have a daughter; you spoke of her." I told her Maggie had died in November. She looked at me, deeply, first with incredulity and then, with the slow dawning of what I had told her, with sadness and empathy. "But you spoke of her as though she were alive."

"In my memory, she will always be alive."

This seems like such an obvious thing. It's what people always say to comfort the grieving. And yet, I'm not sure I got it until now. I thought that it was about keeping the memory of Maggie alive for myself and others. I didn't know that there would be this special place inside me where my daughter will always still be alive and through which others can know and love her as a living person. It seems like magic.

June 7

Thank You Notes

Jim and I were leaving the symphony and ran into some old friends of mine from church. Scott immediately thanked me for the note I had sent them in gratitude for their contribution to the Maggie Feiss Fund. In the first few months after she died, hundreds of people gave both small and large amounts of money to the fund we established to carry on her work.

We chose to house the fund at the Baltimore Community Foundation for many reasons, not the least of which was their quick acknowledgment of gifts, leaving us to write more personal notes as we were ready.

Writing these notes often is painful and tearful, but I am taking it slowly, and I savor thinking about what the person meant to Maggie and what she meant to them.

I still have done nothing about the hundreds of condolence letters I received. They are all in a shopping bag under a table in my office. I reread them as occasions arise, but I don't think I ever will have the energy to reply.

June 8

Vicarious Mothering

When Maggie was around ten, her Aunt Mima, mother of two great boys but longing for a girl of her own, began an American Girl collection for her niece. Mima was extravagant with her gifts, but she said it gave her pleasure to shop for girly things. I understand these days girls collect many of the American Girl dolls, but back then Maggie had just Kirsten, everything for Kirsten! Her Dad even made a simple wardrobe for all the clothes and knick knacks. And I remember her playing endlessly: dressing and undressing, enacting stories, creating social events with her stuffed animals. When we moved from her childhood home when Maggie was thirteen, Kirsten and her small world of stuff got packed into boxes and saved, perhaps for the day when Maggie would have a daughter of her own.

Mima finally got her daughter, and when Jim and I were visiting my brother and his family in January, I found eight year old Marley in her room, playing with her American Girl dolls. "Do you have Kirsten?" Marley said no, but she liked Kirsten. "I'm going to send you Maggie's Kirsten. I know she would want you to have her."

Today I have packed up a box to send north. And so the

circle continues. Now Mima has her girl, and this summer, when I see Marley, she and I will play together with Maggie's Kirsten, and I will be doing the vicarious mothering.

June 9

Too Sad

In April, Jim and I attended a fundraiser at the local library at which authors were in attendance for a meet and greet. As I perused the shelf of books for sale, I immediately landed on *Only Spring, On Mourning the Death of My Son,* by Gordon Livingston. Flipping through, my heart both soared and sank. The book was written in the form of short journal entries, most dated only days apart, beginning with the illness and hospitalization of Livingston's youngest son, Lucas, and, following Lucas's death from leukemia, recording the journey of Livingston's grieving over the next two years. I bought the book and had a tearful (on my part) conversation with Gordon Livingston. It is now seventeen years since Lucas died, and Livingston assured me that the pain will diminish with time.

Last night I started reading *Only Spring*, which Livingston confided never sold well: "It was too sad." His graceful inscription in my copy of the book reads, "To Meg, who understands."

On a completely different note, today is Johnny Depp's birthday. He was Maggie's favorite actor.

June 10

Jealousy

Following Lucas's death, Gordon Livingston dove into a huge fund-raising campaign to subsidize a room in Lucas's memory at the Tremont Plaza Hotel in Baltimore. The Lucas Scott Livingston Suite is a haven where families can stay while their children are being treated at Johns Hopkins Hospital—such a perfect tribute to Lucas and a loving gift to other families who are suffering. Livingston also wrote articles for publication, returned to work, continued to father his teenage daughter, and seemed to be an altogether loving husband to his wife Clare, despite their mutual grieving.

All along in my own journey, I have tried to give myself permission just to do the best I can, but somehow, as I read *Only Spring*, I often feel inadequate and yes, jealous. I finally realized that I was comparing myself and my accomplishments post-death-of-a-child with Gordon Livingston. The Maggie Feiss Fund grows incrementally or in great leaps, but not through any effort on my part. I write, but have no energy or heart for marketing. I don't have to go to work every day. I connect with Stephen often by phone and the occasional visit, but I am not called upon to be there for him on a daily basis. I have Jim taking such good care of me, and he is not suffering the same loss. And I think, "What a slacker!" as my students would say. It's crazy, I know, but there it is.

June 11

And While I'm at it

The true confession is that I have often felt guilty all through the writing of these short pieces about the luxury of my life. How can I even presume that my words might be of comfort to someone who has significantly more weight to bear? The distractions and pleasures of traveling to new places; the freedom from the responsibilities of work or raising children or caring for an elderly parent; the time to read, to connect with friends, to exercise and get enough sleep, and to write here, all these are among my great good fortune. And as I write, I often think how different the experience of grieving a child would be for someone else under different circumstances.

June 12

Public and Private

My old friend Nicki sent me an article, months ago, which I read and put away in my towering pile. Today I discovered it and reread Meghan O'Rourke's meditation on mourning. I was particularly intrigued with O'Rourke's observation that in modern American culture, we do not display our grief. While we have religious and personal rituals, like saying kaddish, usually they do not announce our state of mourning publically.

I remember as a child learning about the old custom of wearing black for a year after a death of someone close and thinking it was a terrible thing. In my mind, wearing black was something that would remind the mourner of her sorrow and perhaps act as a sort of social censure, requiring her not to show joy or have fun. Now, intimate with mourning, I understand that no reminders of the loss are ever necessary and that the social purposes of wearing black surely are more complex.

Lately, I have had a few awkward encounters in which the fact of Maggie's death has come up sort of sideways; that would not have happened if the stranger had known by looking at me that I am in mourning. I also would welcome the lower expectations which might occur if other people were reminded visually that I am not fully myself. Perhaps that decision that others seem to wrestle with about whether or not to say anything about Maggie's death would be eased by the clothes making the statement: I am in mourning, please acknowledge it. On the other hand, the privacy of modern mourning leaves me with the choice: I can keep my grief to myself. I can try to have a normal day.

June 13

Kiwis

Jim bought a big bag of ripe kiwis at the Asian market, and we have been feasting on them. They were Maggie's favorite fruit, and I credit her with my being able to indulge as freely as I do. I used to shy away from kiwis because they were such a pain to peel, but then Maggie learned from her close high school friend, Emily Strauss, the secret of eating kiwis. For the uninitiated, here it is. Cut the kiwi in half. Use a sharp edged or serrated spoon to cut around the edge, just under the skin. If the fruit is ripe, you can do this easily. Pull the skin back so the insides slide out; then slice off the back and presto, kiwi ready to pop in your mouth and savor.

June 14

Energy

As tired as I was a few weeks ago, I have now come a full 180 degrees and am full of energy. I think it has much to do with the long days, a good stretch of sunshine, the fun I'm having with my new quilt project, and Jim and I really appreciating each other. I have been laughing out loud: real, relaxed belly laughs. I have even felt able to make some plans for Maggie's birthday, which is coming up on July 11. Unlike the music fund-raiser, which was such a disaster between Jim and me, this one has been an easy meeting of the minds, for which I am so grateful. In the way of these things, there is a free concert in Catonsville on Sunday, July 12, and it's Deanna Bogart, Jim's and my favorite local blues artist. So we are having an afternoon barbecue here with the extended family, and then encouraging everyone to go to the concert.

June 15

Compassion

I love Anne Lamott's writing and though she is way more California than I, we are kindred spirits. Recently my friend Gina sent me a link to one of Lamott's on-line journals in *Salon* in which she considers grieving. One bit reminded me of something I've been thinking about: "But then you cry and writhe and yell and cry some more; and then, finally, grief ends up being about the two best things: softness and illumination."

I don't feel particularly illuminated by grief, but I am softer. I suppose it can go either way, and I am blessed that I was already starting to know that softening was the best way for me. Then, Maggie's death proved that there is no successful protection against the pain anyway.

I feel more deeply for others. I can look into other's eyes more comfortably. I am more compassionate and, perhaps as a result, I feel people opening more comfortably and easily to me. I'm not sure there is any greater gift from pain than that.

June 16

Four Napkin Rings

I was digging through a drawer, looking for cloth napkins to use with guests, when I came across the small rectangular box with the clear plastic top, under which are nestled four pewter napkin rings. Bill and I were given these as a wedding present, and after the two children were born, we had each engraved with the initials of a member of the family, one for each of us. We were in the habit of having family dinners as the kids grew up, always with cloth napkins, and the napkin rings were a good way not to have to wash the napkins after every meal.

When I moved out in February, 2004, leaving at our home my husband of almost twenty-four years and Maggie, who was in her senior year of high school, I took only a bare minimum of things. I did not want to decimate their lives any more than our decision to separate already had. It wasn't until we had to clear out the house in preparation for its sale the following December that Bill and I faced one wrenching decision after another about what to do with our shared possessions. I don't remember discussing the napkin rings, I think I just took them. I can't say that I have regretted doing so, but these four rings, resting together, still marked: SWF,

MOT, SEF, MOF, are always unsettling and often dismaying whenever I come across them. But I cannot let them go.

When I moved to Jim's house, I again had to make the decision, and again, the napkin rings came with me, this time, carrying even more weight than they had before. We are now down to three, this broken family.

June 17

Journal

I was feeling like I needed a Maggie fix, looked at some pictures and that wasn't doing it, so I went to one of her journals, just flipping through, reading here and there. On one page, the only thing that she'd written: "It's funny how quickly it all goes by." Awww, Mags.

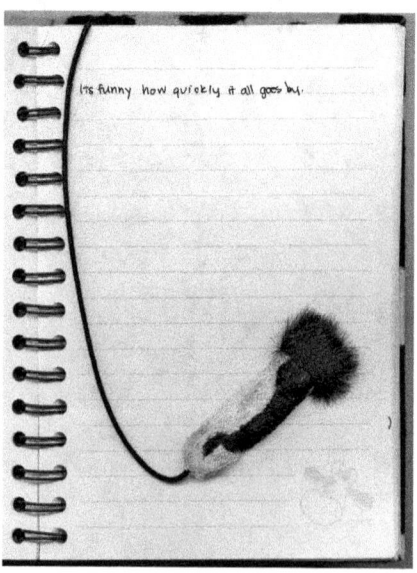

June 18

Hysteria

In the middle of an orgasm, I started giggling, which then turned to laughter, and then hysteria. I have never been so wracked with laughter. It was like the orgasm cracked something open which I couldn't stop. It went on and on. Scary. Funny, but scary.

June 19

Stopped

At the most recent Bereaved Parents group, one mother whose daughter died long ago spoke of how going through pictures became difficult because there was always that moment in the record of her family's life when pictures of her daughter stopped. She brought her hand down and said the word sharply. Tears leapt to my eyes. I had not cried when I checked in with the group, speaking about the memories of Maggie that had come up for me in the past month, but Sadie's pain moved me. I thought of it again today when I took my camera to get prints made of some of my photos from the spring: Phebe and Nora, our trip to Cozumel with Kendal and Janet, lots of loved ones, but no Maggie.

June 20

Prison

I watched a French movie with Helen and Jess: *I've Loved You For So Long*. It was beautifully written and acted; we all loved it, and enjoyed understanding as much of the French as we could before reading the subtitles. In many ways, the movie is about all that cannot be understood between people.

Two moments in the movie struck me. In one, an Iraqi doctor has a photograph of his family on his desk. When his friend picks it up, he pats his heart and says, "They are always here. War is weak. There are some things it can never destroy." Near the end of the movie, the main character, Juliette, says, "The death of your child is a prison from which you can never escape." These two sentiments seemed in opposition. In one, a man, who has lost his entire family to war, is able to find a place in which to love, honor, and cherish them. In the other, a woman succumbs to the devastation by allowing her grief to become a prison. But in the last line of the movie, Juliette says, "I am here. I am here." And, at the end of the day, it is something just to have survived.

Standing at the Edge

June 21

Wild Flowers

It is the summer solstice, a time of year I love. This spring, Jim and I made a wild flower bed in the back yard. I was fearful that the seeds would not take hold because the soil was so bad, but we turned the soil, put down some compost, pulled as many weeds as we could, spread the seeds, and waited. In another display of the tenacity of the beautiful in the face of bare sustenance, we have cosmos, chicory, wild poppies, cornflowers, something that looks like tiny orchids lined along a stem, and more flowers coming. I love them, and so do the bees and butterflies. This bed would make me happy anyway, but added to its beauty is the memory I have of Maggie and me taking pictures of the wildflower garden at the wonderful Eden Project in Cornwall last summer. That was such a good day.

June 22

Black Humor

We have made arrangements for Maggie's name to be placed on the memorial wall at our church but have done nothing with her ashes. I keep the box on the bookshelves that serve as a little shrine in my sewing/yoga/meditation room. Bill, Stephen and I have decided that we'll keep them available so that Maggie's family and friends can take ashes to places that are important to them or on trips to places Maggie wanted to go. We did spread some of her ashes in the garden at her school in York when we were there in December.

So, as I was quilting on this beautiful, breezy first day of summer and the door to my sewing room kept banging, I scanned the room, looking for something small and dense to use as a doorstop and landed on . . . the box of Maggie's ashes. I didn't put that heavy brown cube on the floor and use her "cremains" to hold the door, but I was able to laugh at the sheer practicality of it.

June 23

Confidence

After Maggie's death, I dropped my French class, knowing that my brain was not anywhere close to being able to learn anything other than how to live one day at a time without my daughter. However, I promised my wonderful teacher, Madame Schaeffer, that I would come back when I was able. Now I find myself playing with French again: thinking of vocabulary, practicing saying different phrases and I realize that my confidence is slowing returning and that I feel almost ready to begin again.

June 24

Ganny Memory

I came across a journal entry of mine from June 24, 2001, in which I recorded a sweet memory of Maggie and my grandmother. It was the summer before Maggie and I left for our year in England and, since my grandmother died that year while we were away, it is possibly the last time we saw her. Maggie was almost fifteen and Ganny was 103, confined to a wheelchair and probably unsure about which members of her large and loving family we were, but still very much her wise, wonderful self.

"Sitting in the sun, Maggie and I on either side of Gan, holding her hands. She says, 'We have a nice little group.' Later, peaceful, peaceful, perfect day, warm but breezy, trees rustling, quiet, she says, 'I think we're all going to fall asleep.'

Inside, Maggie comes out from behind the wheelchair she has pushed in for Gan and takes off her sunglasses. Gan says, 'Good to see you.'

Maggie and I, standing together with our arms around each other, getting ready to leave. Gan says, 'It's good to have this . . .' Amen!"

Meg Tipper

June 25

Ram's Head Police

After he heard my eulogy at Maggie's memorial service, an old friend of the family mentioned that he too had had encounters with the "Rams Head Police," saying that they never let him dance there and how amazing it was that Maggie had been able to do what she did. I've seen that "police" person in action myself, and it is one very kind but tough woman whose job is to keep people in their seats so that the people sitting behind them can see the band. When I've needed to move to the music from time to time, I've learned to find little corners to stand and cut loose in.

Last night Jim and I were at Rams Head again to see the Gary Burton Quartet, four very talented jazz musicians, including one of my favorite guitarists, Pat Metheny. It was a great concert and afterwards, while Jim was in the bathroom, I paused to talk to the Police Woman. I told her the story of the Blues Traveler concert last fall and how when Maggie had gone up front to dance, I had said to myself, "They're going to make her sit down." But the PW hadn't, and I wanted to thank her for that. I reminded her of how everyone had been up and dancing for the last few numbers of the show and how pumped my daughter had been. She said it is always a difficult call and she was glad that she'd made the right one that night. Then I told her about my daughter's death just shortly after that wonderful night, and her eyes filled with tears and she hugged me. "What's your name?" I asked. "Maggie."

June 26

Mary Carol, Face to Face

My sponsor is home from China. I have not seen Mary Carol since Maggie died, and they were very close. Maggie was born after I got sober and, especially in her early years when I took her to meetings and everyone knew her, very much a part of my life in recovery. She and Mary Carol had a special bond through acting. Maggie was a drama queen from the start, but as she got older, she found theatre as something she was not only good at but also enjoyed. Mary Carol, a professional actress, always encouraged this interest, and often came to see Maggie in her school plays. She was sort of an acting role model.

So today, at our first time being together, we recalled roles she had seen Maggie perform and other times the two of them had spent together. It felt strange to be going through a first time grieving with someone again. Although Mary Carol and I had spoken and cried on the phone many times, face to face is different. She said, "I can't believe she's really gone," and I realized immediately that I too still have this side of me.

June 27

The Estate

Finally, almost eight months after Maggie's death, her estate is settled. We have been lucky that it was a relatively simple process because of the little that she had, but there were still legal hoops to jump through. We are very grateful that our friend Hacky took care of the whole thing for us.

We did the barest minimum with the funeral home, had Maggie's body cremated, purchased an inexpensive memorial at our church rather than a burial plot, and many people contributed in a variety of ways to help with the expenses around the time of Maggie's death. (For example, Freedom Services, a local company, donated car service for the week, an amazingly kind and generous gesture of support.) And still, the amount in Maggie's estate did not even begin to cover our expenses. Death is a costly business.

June 28

Kill Bill

There were a few financial things which the final distribution of Maggie's estate revealed, which pushed some of my serious buttons around my ex-husband. It so happened that Netflix had delivered the Quentin Tarantino movie, *Kill Bill*, in Volumes 1 & 2, and I found they fit my mood, being about ruthless revenge. However, at the end of the second movie when The Bride tucks her sleeping four-year-old daughter into bed, there I was, sobbing hysterically. And I got clear. All this emotion around the estate is not just plain anger, it's the anger in grief. And that is a fiery anger unlike any other.

June 29

Catbirds

I have always loved catbirds. In fact, they always reminded me of Maggie! They are very talkative and inventive; they are natural performers and love attention, and their tails are so expressive and jaunty!   In the first house Maggie lived in, we had a catbird which we called friendly bird. He would sit on the clothes line or in a lower branch of one of the two silver maples in our back yard and keep me company when I was planting, weeding, hanging clothes, or grilling. We could always count on him showing up when we would gather outside for a summer lunch or dinner at our round picnic table. I remember Maggie delighting in him too.

Now I treasure my catbird visits even more and imagine that Maggie has a voice in all that lovely chatter.

June 30

Reunion Photos

Emily Strauss put photos on her Facebook page from Maggie's high school class's 5th year reunion. I loved seeing those girls having a great time together, and I imagined Maggie in their midst, but did so wish that I could see her smiling face in those pictures.

Meg Tipper

July 1

Alive in my Dreams

I woke up this morning remembering a dream that Maggie and I were in England together. I treasure those moments of lying in bed and holding the feeling of her aliveness.

On another subject, many times I have a feeling of déjà vu, during the day, and I will have the sense that there has been something important from a dream that I can't remember. I don't recall this ever happening before Maggie died. I don't know what to make of it.

July 2

Broken Marriage Bench

It is eight months today. Yesterday Bill and I went to church together to scout out a good location for a bench along the nature trail as a place to sit and be quiet and private in that place. It was a pretty morning, and we agreed easily on a good spot and then worked well together to clear and level it. Then Bill was off to an Orioles game and I to the chiropractor.

Being nothing if not practical and frugal, I originally thought that we could use the bench that Bill and I gave each other for a wedding anniversary present. Then, one day, it was very clear to me that that was not a good plan. Maggie was terribly upset at the dissolution of our marriage and the impact it had on our family, and to use that bench to honor her was not right. So I ordered a new bench, made out of recycled plastic bags, of which Maggie would thoroughly approve. The old bench has a new home at my mother's retirement community, overlooking the pond and the goose with her goslings, neutral territory.

July 3

Face of God

I do not always use the word "God" to name my sense of the divine. It is a word burdened with theology, debate, war, and my own Christian religious upbringing. For lack of anything better, I often use the language of the recovery program, "higher power," or HP for short. Another evolution has been away from any idea about the gender of the divine. To me, this is an absurd discussion, given the infinite and incomprehensible qualities of my higher power. However, I must confess that I have struggled with feeling a deep personal connection with the divine; while I have always believed, I have not always trusted and loved, nor have I always been comfortable believing that I am loved and cared for. There is an immensity about it all that makes such surrender difficult.

Since Maggie died, I have slowly grown into a much more personal relationship with the divine. This infinite and incomprehensible being now has a face, one I love and who I know loves me. And I am absolutely sure that Maggie's spirit is part of my higher power, that she is in it, and they are in me. Some religions would call her an angel, and that seems as good a word as any.

Meg Tipper

July 4

Feeling Good

People ask me how I am feeling these days, and I say "good." I love summer: the long days, warm weather, working in my garden, finding people more relaxed and friendly, flowers, grilling, eating outside, fireflies, driving with the top down, fresh air in the house, bare feet in the grass, mowing at the farm, taking outdoor showers, thunder storms, fresh vegetables from the garden, hanging the clothes on the line. I tell people that I always wanted to be a farm wife, and now, that is my life, in a modest and manageable way.

Maggie continues to be with me all the time, but it's not such a wrenching, heart-broken feeling. She is a comforting companion.

July 5

Road Trip

My dear old friend Diane Purpura and I have hit the road together for a short adventure. Before I ever knew that Maggie and I traveled well together, I discovered a great traveling companion in Diane. Like Maggie, she is easy going and enthusiastic; she travels light in all the best ways.

July 6

Labyrinth

Diane and I are at Kripalu, a yoga retreat in the Berkshire Mountains in Western Massachusetts. It is remote and peaceful here. We arrived after a long drive yesterday, and after dinner, we walked the labyrinth on the south side of the campus. It is lovely at this time of year, with pathways created by white, breathy flowers, interspersed with bright blooms of wildflowers. At the center is a small shrine, created by walkers, with tokens of many kinds: coins, photographs, letters, shells, rocks, small figurines. People have different purposes in walking the labyrinth, but surely for many it is a remembering or honoring walk, to which these offerings testify.

Of course, Maggie was in my thoughts.

It was a long, slow walk through the labyrinth, probably almost half an hour to go in and out. Upon arriving at the end, I turned and was immediately struck that the center, the shrine, was right there. That which had taken me so many steps to reach and return from was right next to me the whole time.

The experience reminded me of the end of the beautiful poem "For Grief" by John O'Donohue, which my friend

Leigh gave me shortly after Maggie died:
> The wound of loss will heal
> And you will have learned
> To wean your eyes
> From that gap in the air
> And be able to enter the hearth
> In your soul where your loved one
> Has awaited your return
> All the time.

July 7

Yoga Dance & Meditation Walk

Maggie only tried yoga once and pronounced it, "the most boring thing I've ever done." So, while I thought of Maggie constantly while I was away at Kripalu, I wasn't thinking how much she would love it. Except for the YogaDance. This was not just yoga with rhythm and music; it was wonderfully playful and freeing, mindful dancing. We connected with our bodies and our breath, the music and the other people in the class. All the rest of the time at Kripalu, I would see another person who had been with me in that class, and we would just grin at the shared memory.

The meditation walk was the last organized activity I did before we left. Our leader, Aruni, invited us to walk with no destination, to be led into the pure mindfulness of walking and being in the world. Rather than the inward experience I had anticipated, I was immediately drawn outwards to notice, really notice, everything: the different shades of green in the privet hedge, the tiny pinecones on the hemlock, the bees clustering around the thistle heads. I also was so open to the calling from the little girl inside who wanted to play: I hop-scotched my way along the patio bricks, slid down the sloped marble beside the stairs, ran across the open grass, and reveled in something I have perhaps not felt since I was a child: the pure freedom of going outside to play. And in all of that, I felt Maggie with me, full of delight and encouragement. She never lost that little girl joy.

July 8

Chocolate Christmas Balls

I drove for four hours in torrential rain across the Mass Pike to drop Diane at Logan Airport and then meet Stephen at Anne Marie and Gregor's house in Gloucester. I already was tense from that drive, and then Stephen and I talked some about how our grieving feels right now, which was good to do, but not easy.

I'm not sure I can blame either of those things for my acting out with food, but after Stephen and I cooked dinner for Anne Marie and she headed back to the art gallery to hang her show, we went on a sugar rampage in a house woefully ill equipped for sweet tooths. We began with a tin of stale chocolate chip cookies, and I even sank so low as to unwrap and nibble the edge of one of the little foil-covered Christmas balls, which had, at one time, been chocolate but had now morphed into something white and rock hard.

July 9

Flat Rocks

Before we left Gloucester, Stephen and I walked down Anne Marie and Gregor's lane to the sea, a place we call Flat Rocks. It is always stark and beautiful there, with the sea churning over the rocks, the lobster pots bobbing on the dark gray surface of the water, sea birds reeling and calling, and, often, as it was today, cold and windy. Still, we stayed awhile, remembering summers when the sun had been shining and the kids had played witch hair with the slippery seaweed, slid into the tidal pools, lay down on the rocks to warm up, and competed at throwing rocks out into the water. Stephen is looking for the right spot to bring some of Maggie's ashes a little closer to him in Boston, perhaps it will be here.

July 10

So Gay

Stephen and I are back in Baltimore, and today we met with Bill and with Tom Wilcox at the Baltimore Community Foundation to discuss our grant-making out of the Maggie Feiss Fund. We collected some ideas from Tom, ran some of our thoughts by him, and then we went out to lunch at the City Cafe to finish making our decisions. The meeting at BCF had been good, but also hard, our first foray into philanthropy out of the gifts given in Maggie's memory. We were ready to relax and laugh.

We took a table outside on an uncharacteristically gorgeous summer afternoon in Baltimore. Shortly after we sat down, our waiter arrived, perhaps the most flamboyant, swishiest young gay man I have ever encountered. We all immediately loved him and had a riotous good time, with all three of us flirting with him. But I know that the unspoken thought between us was that Maggie would have loved him most of all and he her.

July 11

Maggie's Birthday

This day has not always been special in my life, but twenty-three years ago it became so and will always be.

As I lay in bed this morning, I heard Maggie's voice again. She said, "Don't you be sad, Mom" and I smiled.

I have reread the piece I wrote about Maggie's birth. It closes with the following: "You grew inside my body from one minute cell and were delivered to the world in the passion of birth, so universal and yet so special, and now you have begun your journey to become your own person. To call this a miracle is cliché, and yet when are we more awed by God's work and the power of human life than in the moments of birth and death? I love you so much already. Stephen had the only right words, 'Thank you.'"

I learned from Garrison Keillor's wonderful "Writer's Almanac" that today is also the birthday of E. B. White. Maggie, who was an avid reader as a child, loved *Stuart Little* and *Charlotte's Web*. Keillor quotes this saying of White's that perfectly captures much of my daily struggle with life: "I arise in the morning torn between a desire to improve the world and a desire to enjoy the world. This makes it hard to plan the day."

I have had very sweet reminders of the support in my life: a little note from Nicki, phone calls, emails, text messages, all sending love, a card from Maggie's best friend, Jess, flowers from Helen. It all helps, but I have been working hard to stay afloat, on my knees several times, crying, wishing it were different.

July 12

The Birthday Bench

Stephen, Bill, and I met at the church yesterday. Rain had been forecast and it was threatening enough that I took my raincoat, but the weather stayed clear for our dedication of the bench. It was just the three of us with the bench, the mulch, the bricks, the tools, and some of Maggie's ashes, quite a lug along the nature trail.

Our spot still looked good; the grounds committee had cleared a bit more for us, and, best of all, the wild raspberry bushes were loaded with ripe berries. We dug in the bricks and the bench, and then we each took a handful of Maggie's ashes to sprinkle around a bench leg, leaving the fourth unmarked. We cried and hugged, spread the mulch, ate some raspberries, each took a turn sitting on the bench, and cried some more.

Before we left the church, we also lingered at the memorial wall where the plaque with Maggie's name and dates will be placed. It is a beautiful setting. Then, hungry, we caravanned to Highlandtown for the best pizza in Baltimore at Matthew's. It had been a favorite haunt of Bill's and Maggie's, and Stephen and I had never been there. So it was a fitting choice for our birthday dinner.

July 13

Families Together

In honor of Maggie's birthday, Jim and I hosted a barbecue yesterday afternoon with just her immediate family. It was the first time since Maggie's memorial service that this group has been together and the only time since Bill's and my separation that we have had just the two families at any social event. Additionally, at Jim's and my house were Bill's girlfriend Terry, my brother's girlfriend, Liz, and his ex-wife, Cathy! On top of everything, the venue was our house, which is under construction and more than a bit unconventional as a place to host a party. But, it went well: People brought food, ate well, enjoyed the perfect weather, admired my gardens, talked to each other, and seemed to have fun. There is nothing that would mean more to Maggie than to see people she loved loving each other.

July 14

Restless, Irritable, and Discontent

The recovery literature tells us that these are symptoms we should not ignore. I have been all three today. Waking up, I was annoyed at the traffic noise. When people called me in the morning, I was angry about being disturbed. When the phone was quiet all afternoon, I felt neglected. I lectured Jim about not expressing enough appreciation for my help.

Usually I get to four or five meetings a week. Last week, though I was doing lots of yoga and meditation, I was low on meetings. I think there is also the post-birthday let-down. I can push through these events, and then part of me wants to be rewarded with Maggie's return. *Look, I did it, I aced the grieving my dead daughter's birthday test, now can't I please have her back?* This is the first time that I have begun to see the old people-pleasing character defect at work in my grieving. Can I really have been harboring another insane bargain with my higher power that if I do well, I'll get what I want?

I downloaded the pictures from the weekend to Facebook and as I was tagging the people, I wanted there to be pictures of Maggie. I know she was there.

July 15

Curls

My hair is getting long, well long for me. For a few months I have been straightening the wave out of it and then tucking it behind my ears. The last time I got my hair cut though, Karen suggested that I scrunch it after I wash it, let it dry, put on a little product, and encourage the curls. Well, I've never had proper curls before except when I got a perm in the mid eighties, and then they were kind of frizzy. Maggie was the one with the curls, massive curls. But now, if I do what Karen suggested, I have curls too. I shake my head and think, whose hair is this? Did Maggie send me her curls? They make me very happy.

July 16

Ancestors and Children

When a child dies, people say that it is not the natural order of things. I heard this many times, but have never really dwelled on it, thinking that it is an obvious truism and not particularly worth pulling apart. But then Jim and I watched a Disney children's movie called *Mulan*. In it, the characters pray to the ancestors for help with their problems and the ancestor spirits are awakened. They are all wrinkled and wizened and quirky. Ancestors are the ones who came before; they are old before they are dead. Children, on the other hand come after, they are always younger than you and you die before they do. That's how it works.

July 17

This Too Shall Pass

A few weeks ago when I was feeling serene about Maggie's death, a part of me was guilty: *here I am only seven some months since my daughter died and how can I not be all torn up?*, and part of me was cocky: *aren't I the most amazing spiritual giant to be rising above such a loss?*, and all of me wanted to believe that I was going to feel good forever. Now I am back to the more familiar feelings: easily overwhelmed, slightly irritable or outright angry, having difficulty focusing, and sad. And, of course, I am sure that all of these feelings will last forever too.

July 18

Raspberries

It is wild raspberry season. I have always loved berries of all kinds, and, from an early age, Maggie was as passionate about berries as I was. One of her favorite books was Bruce Degan's wonderful *Jamberry*, in which a child and a bear cavort in ever increasing delight among heaps of berries. But always, our favorite was raspberries. Our neighbors had berry canes in their backyard, and we would reach across the fence (and, okay, yes, we would even climb over) and pick berries on summer mornings. Sometimes, we would come to a screeching stop at some wild berry patch along the side of a road and fill a hat or empty coffee cup or whatever we could find in the car. We were raspberry warriors. All of this gave me particular pleasure, because one of my fondest memories is of picking blackberries with my father, who also was a berry fanatic, in the mass of thorny bushes beside the driveway of the house where I grew up.

July 19

One Year Ago

I have often thought that this first year, going through everything for the first time without Maggie, would be the most wrenching. Today, I saw a photograph I took when we were together in England last summer almost exactly a year ago. And I loved that it was just a year ago that we had that special time together. As the reality of a life without Maggie becomes clearer to me, I hold onto that proximity. As time passes, the pain will fade but so also will the immediacy of her, of our time together, even of the memories.

Meg Tipper

July 20

Ghosts

Jim has just bought our recently deceased 99 year-old neighbor's house "as is." We have spent the weekend beginning the immense job of digging out the home of a hoarder. We have begun to remove boxes and heavy-duty trash bags of everything from food and photographs to shoes, clothes, towels, and bedding. We have huge piles of wood, paper, and metal for recycle; we have stacks of books and records for our in-house "yard sale;" we have one room for usable appliances, another for the televisions and stereo consoles which will need to be junked.

It has been the strangest feeling: disrupting this home that slowly closed in on itself as the family dwindled down to one old bachelor alone in the house with all the trappings of his large family stuffed around him. The night after we took possession, I dreamed of ghosts. There was nothing hostile about the feeling, rather I had the sense that the house and the spirits are now able to breathe as light and life and space return. It feels like a way to honor the house for the people who loved it, to give it attention again.

I really don't know to what extent spirits engage with the material world, but if there ever were a house which held the past, it is this one.

All of this is a good distraction. Physical labor occupies my brain, and at the end of the day, there is a huge sense of accomplishment; my body is dead tired and I sleep soundly. Tonight, Jim and I sat on the porch, exhausted, and played a game of checkers with a beautiful old wooden set we found in the house. I was already losing and made what I thought was a good defensive move, which I did not realize set him up for a double jump of my two kings until he looked at me in disbelief and asked, "Can a little one jump a big one?"

July 21

Spider Babies

We have a young man, Mike, helping us clean out the house; he is the youngest son of our realtor, going into his senior year of high school. He has been an awesome worker, hauling heavy, dirty loads downstairs tirelessly. My favorite moment from our work together was when Mike picked up a rolled up piece of paper and jumped as a puff of spider web blew out from inside. We both stared as he held it, dangling, and it shimmered with tiny acrobats. "Spider babies," he whispered. He didn't smash it into the trash bag or toss it to the ground. He held it, marveling. "Would you like to take it outside?" I asked. And he made his way, slowly, downstairs, holding the spiders carefully, like children of his own.

Later, before talking business with Mike's mother, I told her about this moment. It was sweet to share her son's soft side.

July 22

Girls

We have two possible buyers for the house. They are both young couples who love old houses and are dying to find an old Catonsville home they can afford and fix up, the perfect buyers. And, both families have little girls. I imagine living next door to a girl whom I can befriend, spoil, and watch grow up. I know it would not be the same as having my own daughter or my own granddaughter, but it would be lovely.

July 23

Anger and Inertia

Stephen talked to me about how much he hates the summer course he's taking, how much he resents having to pursue his masters degree for recertification, how entirely stupid the teacher is (he refuses to call him a professor), and how he feels it is all a total waste of his time. This is not the first time I have heard this song, but it is the loudest and strongest. In addition, Stephen said that he is having trouble getting off his butt to do anything. I finally asked whether he thought that he was depressed, whether this anger and inertia might be something that he needs some help with. I feel far away and lost about how to help him.

July 24

Mother's Intuition

Since Maggie died, I often have returned to the evening of her death and wondered in amazement how I could not have known: As I showered and changed after an afternoon of working on the farm, as Diane and Annette and I ate a wonderful dinner together at The Helmand and then walked down to Center Stage to see *Who's Afraid of Virginia Wolf?*, as I watched the play, getting twisted up ever tighter in that sick story, as we sat and drank coffee and talked about the play during the first intermission. Never did I have the slightest hint that Maggie had died. It wasn't until I turned on my phone to call Jim during the second intermission and saw a staggering number of missed calls and messages from Bill, that I knew something was wrong.

Since then, I have asked myself over and over again how a mother can not know that her child has died. Wouldn't there have been some commotion in my very being as the fabric of my life was ripped apart? Wouldn't I have felt the vacuum of Maggie's soul leaving this material world? Tonight I was talking to Jim about this and I asked him, "How could I not know?" to which he replied, "How could you know?" And, at the end of the day, I guess that is a more reasonable question to ask, one that is kinder to myself.

July 25

Tiffany

Jim and I are in Chicago en route to a family reunion, but our day of sightseeing in Chicago was greatly abbreviated by my back, which was a mess from four days of too much work in the new/old house. But we were able to take a great architectural boat tour to see the highlights and get a sense of the city's bones. We ended at Navy Pier because I wanted to see the Museum of Stained Glass, but my body was dead tired, and I was feeling a bit unsteady and nauseous. There were no chairs to sit on or benches to lie on in the museum, but I finally found a darkened room with exquisite illuminated Tiffany windows. There was a nook in the wall, and I lay down there, often completely unnoticed by people wandering into the room to look at the windows. Though I was feeling really sick and my back was in knots, lying there and looking at the windows was both inspiring and soothing; they were so beautiful and they also reminded me of a really special day with Maggie.

It was the end of her senior year of high school, and we wanted to do something to thank her good friend, Emily, and her mother, Susan, both of whom had done so much to help Maggie through the trauma, and, yes, drama, of her reaction to Bill's and my separation. The Strauss family dearly loves Baltimore, and so Maggie and I created a Baltimore treasure hunt, taking Emily and Susan to some places we hoped they either had not visited or would love to see again. We included a private tour of the Bromo Seltzer Tower, coffee at the Women's Industrial Exchange, and a movie at The Charles Theatre. A respite in the whirlwind day was our visit to Brown Memorial Presbyterian Church in Bolton Hill to see their newly restored Tiffany windows. None of us had ever seen them, and we loved ambling through that cool, quiet church and admiring the color and romantic artistry of those towering windows.

As I lay on the floor in that room in Chicago, feeling really sick, I tried to breathe and recall the joy in that other day.

July 26

The Himel Family Birthday Weekend

Jim and I have traveled to Madison for his Aunt Mora Himel Lincoln's 100th birthday. It is the first time that Jim's extended family and I are meeting each other, and we have several days worth of events in which to become more familiar. I find myself needing breaks, an hour stolen to read or get away with Jim for a walk. Meeting so many new people and having so many conversations is taxing. I wish I were more like Maggie: outgoing and comfortable in this sort of situation, boundless energy for any social event. There was nothing Maggie liked more than making friends, and she knew how to have fun with people of all ages. In all those qualities, she was very like her father.

July 27

Skip's Shrine

Jim and I are staying with his cousin Jan in Madison. I was eager to meet her as Jim is so fond of her, and I felt a bond as I knew her son Skip died suddenly when he was in his late twenties, about fifteen years ago. It has taken us a few days to open the conversation, but today Jan shared with me about the time around Skip's death, how her other sons had coped, things she had done to mark Skip's birth and death days. Jan is pretty and fit, in her mid-sixties, a successful university administrator; she has loads of friends and is involved in lots of activities. She has a rich and happy life, and she has woven remembering and honoring Skip into the fabric of that life in some beautiful ways. Like my dear friends Anne Marie and Gregor, she has a sort of shrine in the living room with pictures and other things that remind her of Skip.

Right now I have pictures of Maggie all over the house, but my sewing/yoga room is the place where I have collected Maggie's things. The box of Maggie's ashes is there too. It is fine for now, but I think that in time I would like to create a place more central in the house that declares itself as Maggie's space.

July 28

Poo

Having returned home from an intense Himel weekend, today, Jim and I visited my aunt whom I call Doan-Doan, Maggie's godmother. She has been in the hospital and is in constant discomfort, often in pain. And yet she is so thoughtful about checking in with me every few weeks as she did recently with an invitation to lunch. At my place at the table was a paper rose which she said was "special." The card informed me that it was made from elephant poo. This silliness is vintage Doan-Doan and just one reason why she and Maggie bonded so deeply.

I love my visits with Doan because they are unabashed memorials. We always recall funny things Maggie said or did, and I know that we both help each other to heal. This time on leaving though I felt strange, sort of angry, sort of jealous. I couldn't really name it, but I was pretty sure the feeling stemmed from my sense that Doan feels closer to Maggie right now. That is okay and understandable. She is in her late seventies, unwell, and facing her own imminent death. She spends much time thinking, praying, and talking both to God and to Maggie. I know Maggie's spirit has boundless love, enough for all of us who talk to her and miss her. I know that comparisons of quantity or quality trivialize something unique to each of us: the way we hold Maggie in our hearts.

And then amid all this fussing in my mind, I got a good laugh, because I was always a little jealous of Doan-Doan and Maggie's relationship. Here were my own daughter and my dear aunt sharing secrets and enjoying an intimacy that I was left out of. Indeed, I can carry my defects of character into deep grieving as well as the next guy! Poo!

July 29

Fundraiser

We have a contract on the house next door! This has been so smooth that you have to figure it has really good karma. The buyers love the house and want to fix it up slowly. They will settle in two weeks and hope to move in before the holidays. He is a gardener. They have a nine year old daughter who loves my car. The only wrinkle is the pressure it puts on us to clear the house out. The house tour/estate sale fundraiser for the Maggie Feiss Fund that I had toyed with doing sometime in the fall is now planned for August 6!

In contrast to the conflicts with Jim and the other difficulties I felt in March when I considered the concert fundraiser, this event has been an easy collaboration, and I am up to the task of planning it. I feel myself kicking into go mode. It is a great escape.

July 30

This is My Maggie

At a women's twelve step meeting today, Rema was sitting in the row in front of me. Before the meeting started, she came back and sat down beside me, carrying a notebook. I was surprised as we hardly know each other. She just looked at me, opened the front cover and showed me a photograph. "This is my Maggie."

Her daughter is Maggie's age, beautiful; she looks just like Rema. I was so touched by this gesture, by Rema's intuition that her sharing a picture of her alive Maggie with me would not be painful but rather would bring me joy.

July 31

Is This My Receipt?

I was getting some prints from the birthday weekend made at the store where Maggie and I both have gone for prints since before the digital age. As I was paying, I mentioned something about the fundraiser to Tracy, the manager. "What are you raising funds for?" she asked, and I thought, instantly, *she doesn't know*.

I told her about Maggie's death and her eyes filled with tears. She called another sales person over to help the next person in line, and she moved aside to ask me about how Maggie died and to remember her together. Then she said, "I have a twenty year old, and you think you've gotten them through safely . . ." We both locked into each other's eyes, until finally she looked down at the envelope she had been filling out, and then looked back up and shook her head, sort of lost. I reached for the receipt on the counter and asked, "Is this my receipt?" Neither of us could get our heads around returning to the world of a business transaction.

August 1

Shock Trauma

Jim is a forester. He has been tending to trees and wielding a chain saw since he was a kid, helping to clear timber from his father's farm. Still, when he heads out to take down large trees or to prune large limbs, I can't watch. I say, "Isn't there someone who could do this whom I do not love?"

Nonetheless, Jim and two young guys from the neighborhood dove in to clearing the massive growth around the new/old house. He has promised to take care of the tree work as part of the contract, and, of course, that translates into him doing most of the work. I visited a few times, admired the progress, but always left saying, "I can't watch." It reminds me of watching Stephen wrestle in middle school. I went once, saw his body getting twisted up by his opponent, and felt physically sick. I never went again.

So, my worst fears were confirmed when I came home from a meeting and found a neighbor leaving a note on our front door, telling me that Jim had fallen off the ladder and been taken to the Shock Trauma Unit at the University of Maryland Medical Center.

I felt myself constrict. Part of me had that tunnel of

clarity that leads us to do the next thing through a sudden emergency. Part of me felt very surreal, like I had been yanked back into the Maggie nightmare, and I immediately prayed, "God, I know this is a foxhole prayer, but please let Jim be okay because I can't handle this."

Jim is really hurting, his rib is cracked and he has three vertebrae with hairline fractures, but there are no serious injuries. We were incredibly lucky. And yes, I have thanked God.

While we were there, I overheard someone in the next "room" say, "This wasn't what we'd planned to be doing!" and I thought about how every day, millions of people all over the world experience something involving shock and trauma, have their plans drastically altered, and sometimes their whole lives. While I looked at Jim, pale, scratched up, with his neck in a brace, all hooked up with electrodes, and monitors keeping track of his vital signs, I thought how glad I was that Maggie did not die in a hospital, that her end was sudden and on her own terms.

August 2

Nine Months

I have been grieving Maggie's death for the length of time it takes for humans to gestate a new life. But there is nothing ending or beginning today. The day is entirely free, which was not something I did intentionally, but as it turns out, I am glad to have the space to reflect and feel a little. The weather has mirrored my emotional turbulence: storms off and on, thunder with no rain, sun, dark clouds and erratic winds. I have made Jim breakfast, said some prayers, baked some corn bread; I will sew a little, maybe do some gardening if the weather clears or yoga if it doesn't, maybe start reading a new book, maybe watch a movie with Jim. I'll be good to myself, but it still will be another day of missing my baby girl.

August 3

Cape May

My friend Hacky and his family have put their wonderful old Victorian house in Cape May on the market. This is a terrible loss of an emotional centerpiece from their family. For me, there is also sadness because it was in the northeast bedroom on the second floor, in a creaky, old, cast-iron bed that Maggie was conceived. Bill and I had been trying to conceive for over a year, at first sort of a fun frustration, more "trying," but later turning into the fear that at thirty-two getting pregnant was much more challenging than it was at twenty-eight. I remember knowing that I was in the fertility zone and saying to Bill, "If I get pregnant this month, it will be a Cape May baby." Well, whatever it was: the sea air, the relaxation of being away, some sort of Cape May magic worked.

Perhaps it was meant to be that Hacky and Maggie should become dear friends. It was at his home that she came into being, and he always made a space for her to be exactly who she was.

Meg Tipper

August 4

Dancing Queen

I have been accumulating a playlist of Maggie songs; some had significance for us before she died, some have come to have meaning in her death. They make me smile, laugh, dance and cry, sometimes all together. Early in the mix is that quintessential seventies song, Abba's "Dancing Queen." Maggie loved to dance; dancing is what she led me to for my memorial service eulogy, so I see her as a dancing queen. But the song itself carries three wonderful memories from last summer when we were in England. *Mamma Mia!* had just been released in England, and we went to see the movie in York at the City Screen, our favorite movie theatre. It is such a perfect girly movie, and it was all I could do to keep Maggie in her seat, especially for the "Dancing Queen" number. The next day we went for a hike with our friends Tony and Jennie. I had told them that we were going to see the movie, and as we started our drive, Tony said he had a surprise for us. He popped in the *Abba Gold* CD and the first song was "Dancing Queen." He cranked up the volume, and we all sang. Finally, a few days later, Mags and I joined our friend Tracey, her partner Sarah, and a friend of theirs at a traditional English country fair. As we walked to the fairgrounds from our parking spot, we passed an old calliope and the tune it was playing: "Dancing Queen!" Maggie and I looked at each other and said, that's three, making it our official theme song for the trip. So, I hear that song, and it floods me with the joy of those memories and the sadness of not having my daughter to dance with.

August 5

Weary

I have been emotionally flat lately, kind of wrung out. I have to force myself to write, always tempted to conclude that I have nothing to say that I can put words to. There is a developing weariness to my grief, no longer fresh and interesting, just a tiresome, uninvited guest.

August 6

Talking with the Dead

Recently I have finished rereading Marianne Wiggins' brilliant novel, *Evidence of Things Unseen*. It was my recommendation for my new book club, and as I was flipping back through the book, seeing what had grabbed me as I read, I found the following passage I'd underlined, describing Opal's state of mind as she thinks about where to spread her father's ashes: "She wondered how to say 'goodbye'—but then she understood that thinking about what to say was another way of saying it. That thinking about what to say was something that would be ongoing for the rest of her life—the ongoing soliloquy inside one's mind that sounds like talking with the dead" (221).

I suppose that humans are the only animals to have an internal narrative, to think about our life as we are living it. I've heard we are the only animals to have a consciousness of our own impending death. And rereading this passage, I think about how this talk that goes on in my head has changed since Maggie died. Certainly the field of vision is bigger, wider and deeper, and yes, my thoughts go more to her, my constant companion.

August 7

Merry Christmas Buzzy

Yesterday was the first fundraiser event. Jim and I have been going flat out, but we were ready, and the house looked great. I actually felt like it was breathing, stretching, welcoming the presence of people having a party. I think even old crusty Otto was giving us his blessing, because he made a contribution! As I was standing in the master bedroom, talking to Diane, I spied a piece of paper sticking out from under the wardrobe. By now everything is pretty clean, so I bent down and pulled the paper out. It was one of those Christmas money envelopes with Merry Christmas Buzzy (Otto's family nickname) written on it. Inside was a crisp $10 bill.

I loved the balance of the event because we met everyone as they came in, had a few moments to really connect, and there was always a sense of remembering and missing Maggie. After that, they had time to wander through this amazing house at their own pace and with their own thoughts. Then, they brought us their treasures and sat outside and had some food and chatted, met each other. And once again it was a beautiful evening—cool and clear. I think Maggie enjoyed her party.

August 8

Shameless

My plan had always been to let people shop at our indoor "yard sale" and then to ask for donations. Jim argued that for people who don't have any connection to Maggie, this system was not going to yield much money, that buyers would take advantage and give less than we would ask for. I held my ground; I just had a feeling about it. I made sure that Bill picked up more of the brochures from the Baltimore Community Foundation. There we were: I sitting behind a card table with my cash box brimming with cash and checks, Maggie's beautiful face shining from the front of the brochure. People would invariably approach with the classic yard sale question, "What do you want for this?" And I would smile, look up into their eyes, and say, "It is up to you. Decide what you think is fair and make a donation to the fund we created in memory of my daughter who died in November. Here, you can read about her and the fund." They were helpless.

Perhaps ten people in two days gave less than I would have hoped to get. Everyone was so generous. Many people stopped to read the brochure right there and to say how amazing Maggie was. Some asked to hear more about her.

Some told me their stories of people they had lost. It really was a rare and special sort of yard sale!

August 9

Six Degrees of Separation

I had three of these in one day yesterday. The first two happened at the general yard sale, the final event in our fundraising triathlon. The first early bird arrived at 7:15 for the 8:00 opening. I introduced myself and he said, "Oh, my wife's name is Meg." "Margaret?" I asked. "Yes, she's the sixth generation of Margaret in her family. And we have a daughter named Meghan." I stood there with my mouth hanging open. In my almost fifty-seven years of life with this name and this story, I have never heard of another woman with the same tradition and . . . she's a Margaret too. It felt both strange and wonderful, because my name carries so much weight and significance for me, and here was another woman whom I can share that with. I will call her, just to connect. My early birder also took some great stuff and wrote a really generous check. A little later, a young man showed up with his girlfriend. He had heard about the sale from Stephanie, Maggie's dear friend whom she called Seb, who had been at the Thursday night event, with whom he works on the water taxi. We figured that he must have driven Maggie to and from Locust Point last summer. In addition, when he was a kid, the house we were cleaning out was on his newspaper route. He remembered quirky old Otto Stude and his house full of newspapers.

Finally, in the evening, Jim and I went to a party. There we met a couple whom I did not know, but who had known Maggie because their son is best friends with a boy Maggie used to babysit. We ate dinner together, and not only have they also lost a child, a son, but another of their sons, Taj, was best friends with Anne Marie and Gregor's son, Galen, and was at Simon's Rock with Galen when he was murdered.

It is a powerful reminder of what I felt so strongly just after Maggie died: that we all are connected, all part of one family, that the spirit energy of that is powerful beyond our limited comprehension, but also that the human energy of connection can be really powerful too.

August 10

Dragging

It is now two days after the conclusion of all the fundraising events. I had expected to be tired yesterday, but was surprised that today I was still dragging my ass around. It wasn't until this afternoon that I acknowledged to myself that this past weekend had been emotionally as well as physically taxing. I don't know how I can get so disconnected from myself as to miss that obvious fact, but I do.

Plus the house next door is empty. This occupation that has been so all consuming for a month is behind me, and I have four days before leaving for the family vacation. It is in that down time when feelings can overwhelm.

August 11

Vintage Clothes

On the day of the yard sale, a beautiful young woman who looked to be about twenty-seven, landed on the porch like a butterfly. She had on a lovely, fitted, 1950s dress with two-inch, black pumps. I went through my spiel about everything being a donation to Maggie's Fund and handed her a brochure. "Are you interested in the vintage clothes?" I asked. She smiled, nodding, and I directed her upstairs to the cedar wardrobe in which I had arranged all the worthwhile clothing I had found in the house. A bit later she arrived with several items to buy, and I asked if she had a business. She did, an online shop, and because I liked her immediately, I invited her back the next day to see some other clothes, things I had been saving from my grandmother's house.

We had the best time! It was a girl fest of holding up one garment after another, imagining my grandmother in her twenties in the 1920s, so slim and chic, after the war, before she was married, going to parties in these beautiful dresses, and treasuring the fact that she had saved them, reminders of the time in her life when she was young and carefree. Many of the clothes were badly damaged, but Cristen said she loves to do hand sewing and could make the repairs. There were other clothes, now very fragile, which my grandmother had saved from before her time, and Cristen said she would send these to auction to go to people who do costuming and museum purchases. It made me so happy to share these treasures with someone who appreciated them and to think that they might bring in some more money for Maggie's Fund.

As we finalized the transaction, I asked Cristen about her life and found out that the business is something she does on the side for fun and to make money. She is close to the end of her PhD at Penn in neurology and will move to Baltimore when she is finished to be with her boyfriend who is in residency at Johns Hopkins. Her research has included some involvement with the implants which can interrupt seizures. I told her that we had just decided to give a considerable gift from Maggie's Fund to CURE, the organization which supports Epilepsy research.

As Cristen left, we made plans for an outing to Ellicott City after she moves to Baltimore. We will poke around in the vintage shops there and have a coffee, and I hope I will get to be friends with another promising young woman, one who might help find a cure for the terrible disease that stole Maggie's life.

August 12

Greatest Fear

In twelve step recovery, the fifth step involves talking with another person about our "moral inventory." Yesterday I heard a fifth step inventory from someone I sponsor. It is always a privilege to be so trusted, and I always learn some things about myself as I listen to someone else tell her darkest secrets.

My sponsee knew Maggie and certainly knows my pain around this loss. When she arrived at the section of her inventory when she talked about fears, she confessed that her greatest fear is of losing one of her children. There was, of course, nothing to say. It is every mother's greatest fear. We both welled up with tears, and I took her hand. "I'm sorry to make you sad," she said.

August 13

Living Vicariously

The soon to be new owners of the house next door have already contracted to have the wallpaper removed and plaster skimmed in the house. Yesterday, we took over some ice for the guys to cool their drinks down on the hottest day of the summer so far this year. The head guy **Bill** had a strange way of speaking; I couldn't really identify what was wrong.

Today he brought by some fresh muffins in a white baker's box tied with string. He said he wanted to express his appreciation for the ice and that he had brought muffins because he misses being able to eat them himself. Since developing throat cancer, he makes gifts of the foods he loves but can no longer eat so that he can live vicariously.

I was so touched and thought immediately of the way I now devour other people's twenty-something children and how I feast in the presence of mothers and daughters enjoying each other's company.

August 14

Paupac

Today we begin our week at Lake Paupac in the Pocono Mountains of Pennsylvania. Paupac has been our family's summer home since I was a child. We have never owned property here, and there was a gap of about fifteen years during which we did not come, but all in all, this has been our special place. First it was my extended family of grandparents, aunts, uncles and cousins on my mother's side who gathered here for a week or two of having the family together beside this beautiful glacial lake. Now, it is my mother, siblings, their spouses or partners, and my children, niece and nephews who treasure the few days when we can all steal away from our respective responsibilities to remember how simple life can be and how much we love each other.

Whenever someone is missing from Paupac: for camp, early soccer practice, summer travels, a work conflict, we feel their absence. When the family picture is taken, we hold up a sign with his or her name. This summer, we all will be here, even Bill is coming for a few days, and we all will be missing, missing, missing Maggie. As we got ready to go this morning, I felt anticipation and dread, another one of many confusing times of strong, conflicting feelings. A few days ago, I was talking about Maggie with a friend and I began to cry. She asked, "I'm sorry, I didn't mean to make you cry. Is it sad or good?" "Sad and good," I said.

August 15

Head Lice

My niece, Marley, picked up head lice at summer camp, just like Maggie did. Though her hair is not curly, otherwise it is as thick and luscious as Maggie's was. I have this sick feeling when I watch my brother comb through Marley's hair, looking for nits. I really think I may have something like post traumatic lice stress disorder from the two times Maggie had head lice. Each was a horrendous infestation; I mean the lice had found the five-star lice hotel and they were not leaving! Trying to comb through Maggie's hair was impossible, plus her hair had a certain texture which enabled the nits to cling tenaciously. Finally, the only recourse was to slide the nits down each strand of hair with my fingernails. We spent hours and hours doing this, with the smelly shampoo burning her scalp and my fingers. The second time she had them, I came a hair's breadth away from shaving her head. I still have head lice nightmares!

Most of the time I am grateful for whatever memories of Maggie life brings me, but this one I'm pretty sure I'd like to lay to rest.

August 16

Trip to the Falls

We almost always make a trek to the waterfall which crashes into a deep pool about a mile downstream from the outlet of the lake. Jim, Charlie, Stephen, Marley and I set out with Mom. Though the walk down is rocky and rooty and, in places, quite steep, my Mom always accompanies us. I think it is a symbolic accomplishment for her. Last year Maggie was with us and this year she isn't. I held all the feelings as we made the pilgrimage: joy that Stephen is with us, even for a short weekend, amazement and gratitude that my mother is still here and still able, at 82, to walk to the falls, and a wracking emptiness that not even the chatter of my sweet niece and the tearful hug of my youngest brother could fill.

Standing at the Edge

August 17

Birthday Hats

We celebrated my brother Charlie's fiftieth birthday with a family dinner. The food was prepared for us and we ate at the lodge, but otherwise, everyone pitched in to make it a festive event. There were many highlights: Charlie's face when he saw the balloons and the table all decorated and the family gathered for him, my mother, sitting beside her baby who is 50!, Charlie's eldest son Jack enjoying telling stories about his Dad, my brother Bill reading his poem, which was both a roast and a love poem, our hearty and rousing singing of Happy Birthday.

But, for me, the hats were the biggest fun of all; they were, I confess, my idea. I had bought four for Charlie's family members, who had been stymied on their bringing hats because of the head lice infestation. As I bought the gold top hat and the purple pimp hat and the black blues brother's hat and the big straw Mexican hat, I had Marley, Jack, Mima, and Willy in my mind's eye respectively. But the party organizers had laid all the unclaimed hats out on a table and let anyone who needed one pick. Lo and behold, each one went right for the hat I had imagined him or her in. Everyone looked silly, and we were all a little transformed by our hat identities. I thought about how much Maggie would have loved the whole party, but especially this opportunity to dress up and perform.

At one point in the evening, Kendal asked me if I was okay and I had to apologize that I had been a million miles away. I can't say that I was thinking about Maggie, I don't remember having anything particular on my mind. I just wasn't there. Part of me wants to beat myself up any time I check out and am not present for the gifts of my life. Another part is more understanding of my need to detach from the buzz, to go inside and take a breath.

August 18

France

Kendal and Janet and my Mom are leaving Paupac to travel to France to visit my mother's sister, Sally. I am happy for them to be having this time together. It is not only Maggie's death; it also is the number of our mother's friends who have died this year, both have made all four of us keenly aware that we need to seize the days for adventures with our intrepid mother.

August 19

Bribery

I knew I wanted to spend some quality time with my niece and each of my nephews. Marley has been easy because she initiates: inviting me to paint our toenails together, to go swimming, to play a game of pool. However, the boys, all of them in high school, are more of a challenge, and I know, given the choice, they would rather be doing almost anything other than hanging out with their old Aunt. However, I do have cunning on my side and lots of experience with teenage boys. I brought gifts for each of them and told them that I will be happy to give them their present after we spend some time doing something together. Pure unadulterated bribery has always been part of my parenting repertoire.

Yesterday Jack and I baked blueberry pies together, and I taught him to cut in butter for the crumble for the topping. I promised him that it will be a skill with which to impress girls. Then Jack took me out for my first time in a kayak. I was not very adept and kept dripping all over myself, which he found mildly amusing and a little pathetic. But we did have a very good paddle across the lake and down into the inlet. Once we were out of the wind and began our more quiet progress into the inlet river, Jack began talking about his Maggie tattoo, which seems to be his way into the subject of Maggie. I asked if he thinks about Maggie sometimes and he said yes. After we turned around in the inlet and were just floating out, we were quiet. The bottoms of the kayaks dragged across the aquatic grasses, wind stirred the treetops, birds called from the woods, and Jack and I floated, peaceful in our little boats.

Later, we received rave reviews on the pies. Here is the recipe:

Fresh Blueberry Streusel Pie
    8 oz sour cream (can use ½ plain yogurt)
    ¾ c sugar (can use ½ brown)
    1 egg
    2 T flour
    1 t vanilla (can use ½ almond extract)
    ¼ t salt
    2 ½ c fresh blueberries
    1 unbaked 9" pie shell

Combine everything except blueberries and beat for 5 minutes until smooth. Fold in berries. Spoon into unbaked pie shell. Bake at 400 for 25 minutes.
    3 T flour
    2 T sugar
    3 T chopped pecans
    3 T butter

Cut butter into flour, sugar and pecan mixture until mix resembles course crumbs. Sprinkle over pie and bake for 15 minutes more.

August 20

Death Goes On

I have just finished reading the delightful book *The Guernsey Literary and Potato Peel Pie Society*. It is an epistolary novel, so Shaffer sets herself the difficult task of achieving many believable and distinct voices for the narrative. I understand that she was a natural oral story teller, so perhaps this skill came more easily to her than it would to others. Shaffer died in 2008, which makes me so sad, because I want to read more by her and this is her only published work.

In any case, one of my favorite characters, Amelia, writes in one of her letters about losing her son during WWII: "When my son, Ian, died at El Alamein . . .visitors offering their condolences, thinking to comfort me, said, 'Life goes on.' What nonsense, I thought, of course it doesn't. It's death that goes on; Ian is dead now and will be dead tomorrow and next year and forever. There's no end to that. But perhaps there will be an end to the sorrow of it. Sorrow has rushed over the world like the waters of the Deluge, and it will take time to recede. But already, there are small islands of—hope? Happiness? Something like them, at any rate."

I think about the differences between losing a child in the middle of a war, when so many people are grieving their own losses and the entire world is upside down, when people have little patience or energy for others' pain. To hear a friend say, "Life goes on," is a kind of dismissal that I never had to face, thankfully. Because of course, noticing and embracing life is the place one needs to find in order to emerge from the sorrow, but no one could have forced me to get there, and, given my contrary nature, any such nudging would inevitably have set me back, I'm sure, because in fact, death does go on, even during peace time.

August 21

Ankle Bracelet

I was putting away the few pieces of jewelry that I brought to Paupac when I found an ankle bracelet that I bought with Maggie when we were in Jamaica together in 2006. I wore that anklet the whole vacation and then pulled it out again and wore it for most of the summer in '07. I always felt the need to do something a little extra hip when I didn't have to work. When we went out West, Maggie and I each got a braid with beads woven into our hair and I kept mine all summer, another year it was a collection of knotted thread bracelets Maggie had made for me. Each summer thing was just a chance to be a little bit young, a little bit girly, with my daughter. So, I happily fastened the beads around my ankle and am wearing them with a smile.

August 22

Continuing Education

I was taking French at the community college last fall and pulled out of the class when Maggie died. Since then, I have felt overwhelmed at trying to find the right words in English, let alone navigate a long lapsed foreign language. However, I love my teacher and do still want to nurture myself back into speaking French more fluently, and Jim has urged me to go back and try again. So, I have resolved to do so. When I talked to Madame Schaeffer, my wonderful teacher, and confessed my fears at not being able to do much, she laughed, "Meg, this is continuing education. We are here to have fun!" Of course, I need to remember that I don't have to be perfect, that I can just do the best I can and have fun. This is the message of my life, over and over again: continuing education!

August 23

Loose Ends

My friend Beth came for a visit this morning, the last day of her summer vacation before returning to her job as a first grade teacher. I remember always having a sense of desperation about these days, wildly trying to finish up everything I would have no time for once school started. It was a kick butt time, getting ready for teaching, for the kids returning to school, and for the much more demanding pace of my life during the school year. There was never a question of what to do, just what to do first.

Now I am home from Paupac, but not gearing up for school. Last year, my first year of retirement, I was simply elated at the sense of freedom. Now, I have no wish to be returning to the classroom, but I do have a strange, wobbly feeling of loose ends, as though some things should be tied up, but I have no idea what they are.

August 24

Sumac

The sumac is turning red. There is a desperate fullness in the chirp of the crickets. The heads of the sunflowers are drooping, and most of the flowers are on their way to being picked clean by the birds. I'm harvesting the last of the tomatoes and getting ready to plant the fall garden crops: spinach, kale, parsnips. The light comes later in the morning; the sun casts a longer shadow. I take stock of these signs of summer waning and know that on the other side is fall, always the season of death for poets, and now, also for me.

August 25

Healing

While I was at Paupac, I tried to jump into the base of the falls, but misjudged the distance and instead landed one ass cheek on a rock before sliding into the churning water. As I swam away, I tested movement and judged nothing to be broken, but knew that I would have one hell of a bruise. Now, a week later, I have a purple bruise covering about seven inches of my left butt and thigh. Jim says it looks like a tattoo gone very wrong. The good news is that it is healing—I can sit more comfortably, walk less awkwardly. It is beginning to itch a little. The bad news is that the hematoma is still quite large and my medical consultations, which have involved dropping my pants fairly indiscriminately, suggest that I may have a hard but tender mass under my ass for quite some time.

Then today, I spent time with my friend Paula who is recovering from two broken bones in her leg. She had surgery to reconstruct the bones and now has a metal bar near her ankle, a huge black boot she straps on to protect her lower leg when she goes out for physical therapy, a walker, and a wheelchair. She also has Eben, her dear husband, who has nursed her tirelessly and affectionately for six weeks. Today,

I got to see a serious injury, one requiring multiple layers of intervention and support to repair and heal. Sometimes, the body cannot take care of everything itself.

And so I am led to think about bruising and breaking, then, if we're lucky and everything is working right, of healing, as the body clears away the damage and becomes whole again. Slowly, slowly.

August 26

Are you Sure you Want to Delete MOF Medical?

My financial software records categories for expenses and offers up options which it predicts might be correct. Today, it gave me "MOF Medical." At one time that was a frequent category, but now, for better or worse, I have no need for it. There are other offenders: MOF clothing, MOF travel, MOF education, MOF gifts. So today I went into Quicken and cleaned out all those categories. Each deletion was followed by a little box which asked, "Are you sure? If so, type in *yes*." Ironic that Quicken gave me warning and checked with me before getting rid of my daughter. Now, the only category left is Maggie Memorial.

August 27

Lost

Several people have told me lately that they can't believe that I am retired, that they can't imagine me not teaching, don't I miss it, etc. Last year, I was overjoyed not to be going back to school at the end of August. Jim and I were taking off for a magical two weeks of hiking and exploring in the northwest, and I was enjoying the freedom in the moment. Later in the fall, we spent two weeks with family and friends in Japan, and students and grading could not have been farther from my mind. Then Maggie died and suddenly teaching wasn't even on my radar. I was so grateful not to have to accomplish anything significant.

But now, at the end of this August, even though we will leave on another great trip in a few days, I am feeling lost. Part of it is that my life without Maggie has a chronically unmoored feeling. *Where can I rest in this churning emptiness where Maggie is supposed to be?* Inevitably, the mind will turn to work as a safe harbor. Yesterday I mentioned this to Jim in a casual way, and he said, "So your body just wants to be making lesson plans?" and I burst into tears. It was the truest thing he could have said. There is something almost instinctive about this teaching rhythm in my body.

August 28

First Job

It was hot today and my friend Helen invited us over for a swim. Her daughter Jess has just been hired for her first job out of college, so we were hanging out around the pool, hearing about it all. She starts on Monday. I was grateful that I had known this moment with Maggie. Last fall, because her seizures were out of control, Maggie knew she couldn't look for a real job, so she decided to interview with the volunteer coordinator for Living Classrooms Foundation. They had a two hour lunch, connecting around all sorts of things that they were both enthusiastic about and that Maggie could possibly become involved with. A few days later, they offered Maggie a job. "We know that there are some health issues, but we want you on our team. You can work as you are able." It was the most amazing gift, and Maggie was riding high, both on the affirmation of her capabilities even with epilepsy, and also on the good she would be able to do. It also was a relief to Bill and me; we had had so much fear for her as we watched Maggie's post college life close in on her.

As we left, Helen and Jess were getting ready to go out for a celebratory dinner, and I tried not to be jealous. That I didn't get to do.

August 29

Blake and Tanya

A young man at Kinkos was a huge help to me in getting some images sized for the quilt I'm making; it was a fairly time consuming and exacting process. He didn't have a name badge, so I asked him and he told me, "Blake."

Later, I saw a small, delicate tattoo on top of his wrist: "Tanya."

"Do you still love Tanya?" I asked.

"She's my mother," he replied with a little smile.

"Then you'll love her forever," I said, "Is she still alive?"

"No," and we exchanged the look.

"I have a memorial tattoo for my daughter."

"That must have been hard," he said.

"It still is; it will be hard forever. It's always hard when we lose people we love. How old were you when your mother died?" I asked.

"This age."

"So this is all recent." He nodded. "I'm so sorry. You need to take care of yourself."

"I'm trying," he said.

When we were all done, we shook hands. "Where do I

pay?" I asked.

"Have a good day," Blake said. Thinking he had misunderstood me, I repeated my question. And Blake repeated, "Have a good day."

"Really?" I asked. He smiled and nodded. "Thank you. Thank you very much," I said.

As I left the store, the tears flooded up. I was overwhelmed by our connection and by his thoughtfulness and generosity. Tanya, you have a good boy.

August 30

Traveling Again

Jim and I were supposed to leave to go diving in Bonaire on November 7, 2008. There was even a brief time when we still considered going, just getting away between Maggie's death and the memorial service. But as much as I longed for escape, I knew there would be no solace or even pleasure in taking the trip that we had planned. We cancelled and were able to reschedule for this last week before Labor Day, a good time to get away.

Taking off for Bonaire inevitably brought the days after Maggie's death rushing back, and, just to add further drama, Bonaire is a place I have been to before, diving with a former boyfriend. Further proof that I can run, but I can't hide.

August 31

Weightless

After we arrived and unpacked, we grabbed tanks and dove right out from the hotel. With a shore dive, the transition into and out of the water is tricky: slippery and rocky underfoot, wobbly with the motion of the waves, and, for someone small like me, difficult to stand and walk with the weight of all the gear. There is that magic moment going in when I can sink down and feel the water take the weight. However, at the end of the dive, the difficulty is multiplied, trying to stand and balance on tired legs and lift the tank out of the water.

There is the parallel with grieving: the relief of giving up and letting myself be buoyed and the effort required when I take up the weight of the pain again and again.

September 1

Happy as I Can Be

At dinner, Jim and I were talking about my work. He said he wondered if maybe I need something to "sink your teeth into." When I pressed him, he said it's not about the money but rather a sense that with all I have to offer: training, experience, expertise, that I might want to be more involved in something worthwhile.

I have been most grateful not to have the stress and demands of anything that requires, "teeth." That I can spend a day staring into space with no one having to pick up my slack is a great luxury and blessing. But it is possible that I am getting more ready for something. I don't know. I did tell Jim that this past year, I have been as happy and fulfilled as I can be, under the circumstances.

September 2

Maggie Attack

I was standing onboard the Golden Eye as we motored to our second dive site. I love the feeling of the wind and the sun. I saw flying fish, which always make me happy. Suddenly, I felt that terrible, breath-taking stab of pain, the one that used to grab me so often in the early days of grieving, the one that chokes all the life out of me with its stark announcement: Maggie is dead. I felt my legs go weak and the tears leap to my eyes; I fought to catch my breath. There was no reason for this. It was almost like something in me wanted to sabotage my happiness. I sought out Jim and put my arms around him and nestled into his shoulder. He held me, even though I know he felt hot and sticky in the Bonaire humidity. "Thanks, darlin'" I said when I could speak, "I had a Maggie attack." "Those happen," he said.

September 3

Dead Dead

Last night I asked Jim how he thinks of Maggie now that she is dead. He got that glint in his eye and said, "In a cloud with little wings and a halo, flitting around, doing her angel thing." "No, really," I said. Then he went into this long riff about memories and then about DNA, none of which I really followed because I was getting the drift and not liking what I was hearing. "So, what you're saying is that when you're dead, you're dead. That's it." "Yes."

I know many people who do not believe in any afterlife. I do. I don't usually feel threatened in my beliefs by someone else's non-belief. So, why did I get defensive, and yes, truth be told, angry at Jim's credo? Part of it may be that my signs and senses of Maggie feel fragile, always teetering on the edge of my own skepticism. Part of it may be that Jim has always been so supportive of my beliefs—my prayer life and meditation time, my going to the psychic and the medium, my stories about times I feel Maggie's presence or hear her voice. I have sensed in Jim a depth to his own spirit that belies his claims to non-belief. But then, I wonder if this too is simply my projection, my wishful thinking, and I feel confused and disappointed. Poor Jim. He told me what he really thought, just as I asked him to, and I got angry and distant because it wasn't what I wanted to hear. I apologized later. He is a very patient man.

September 4

Pretty Woman

I came into the hotel room after a swim and Jim was stretched out on the bed, watching *Pretty Woman*. I'm sure he was actually just flipping through that channel as one of twenty he was watching, but I flopped down on the bed next to him, saying, "OH, Maggie and I loved to watch *Pretty Woman!*" Bless him, we watched the whole glorious movie, from Julia Roberts singing "Kiss" with Prince in her bath, out of tune with her headphones on, (second only to Eddie Murphy's "Roxanne" scene in *48 Hours*) to Richard Gere climbing the fire escape. I so appreciated Jim doing that for me, but we both knew I was missing Maggie, missing catching her eye and smiling or saying the line in those moments we both always relished, like "big mistake!" or "Cinder-fucking-rella!"

September 5

There is No Ending

With us in Bonaire is a couple from Baltimore who also had to cancel their trip from the same week last fall. They told us their son had run into difficulty at college. Towards the end of our week of diving together, I broached the subject again, asking how their son is doing now. He is in a new school, which he loves, and he is doing well academically, has made up the credits he lost in the fall, and seems to be on track. I said I was so glad that there has been a turn around, a happy ending.

But then I got to thinking about all the challenges of parenting, that except for death, there is no "ending." There is always more to the story. Our children's lives are full of so much that is treacherous, there is so much that can go wrong.

We met another couple diving whom we like very much and we had dinner together last night. In the course of getting to know them better, I learned that two of their three daughters have a serious health condition, which greatly compromises their lives and for which they each have had multiple surgeries. I saw in James and Rosaria's eyes the pain of walking side by side with children whose health is unstable, the fear that they could lose one or both of their daughters, the anger about their children's unrealized potential, and the admiration for their daughters' courage and perseverance.

I wish them all happy endings.

September 6

Desktop

I booted up my computer after having been away for a week and therefore saw my desktop photograph with fresher eyes. The sun is setting behind mountains with the red sky reflected in the sea. In the foreground, a deer grazes under a tree next to a little lamp with a top like a tiny Japanese temple. Jim and I had just disembarked from a beautiful sunset ferry ride to the small island of Miyajima, Japan. He had told me about the tame deer there, but somehow, I had not imagined that they would be roaming everywhere. This picture so captures that moment, but the most treasured aspect is the eyes with which I saw the scene. As we traveled for those two weeks in October with Jim's two sons and their wonderful girlfriends, connecting with Jim's friends and family in Japan, a dream trip really, Maggie was home, living with Bill, living. I stood in that moment with no tinge of longing, no sadness tugging at the edges of my happiness. What parent can ever appreciate that luxury until it is gone?

September 7

Maggie's Graduation Present

Greg Otto is an artist who loves Baltimore as Maggie did. Maggie and I both have long admired his bright, bold renderings of some of the city's most distinguished architectural features as well as his eye for the more subtle nuances of color and detail in portraying more humble parts of our city and her people. I wanted to give Maggie an original work of Greg's for her college graduation present and spent several very enjoyable weeks looking at work in Greg's home studio and chewing on my choices. Unexpectedly, I kept coming back to a work which was not a cityscape at all, but rather a whimsical oil of a 45 rpm record, done on a round canvas, about 18 inches in diameter, in bright orange, green, and white. The record is a Fox label of "Bad Bad Guitar Man" by the Larados. Everything about it made me happy. I bought it, and on the card I wrote, "May 2008, Dearest Mags, You are five star and platinum gold! I'm always proud of you, but especially right now. I hope you'll put this art on your wall, that it will make you smile and remind you of me and how much I love you. Always, Mom XOX"

I have not been able to hang this wonderful art, though Jim and I have several of Greg's pieces in our home and love his work. I feel like this one doesn't belong to me. Recently I figured out what I am supposed to do with it. Maggie wants me to give it to my dear old friend Hacky, who has no children and who had such a special friendship with Maggie. He has just set out to create a new partnership, a law firm, in a new office space, and Maggie wants that happy art hanging on the wall there, reminding him of her and how much she believes in him and loves him.

September 8

You Look Sad

After a twelve step meeting, Timmy, someone I am comfortable with but whom I don't know well, came up and said,

"Are you okay?"

"Yeah, I'm fine," I said, nodding, smiling.

He tilted his head, "I glanced at you during the meeting and you looked sad."

I felt the tears coming. "Well, you know," I said, "I am sad a lot of the time, missing my daughter, it's tough."

"It is," he said, "impossibly sad and tough."

I was crying, and he did not seem to mind. He cleared a place for me to be sad with him, and it was a gift.

September 9

The Writing Nudge

Two things happened yesterday to invite the writer in me out to play. First my friend Rafael told me that he is fiction editor of a small literary magazine and asked me to send him a story. Secondly, and completely coincidentally, I had scheduled a coffee with my friend Meghan, herself a fiction writer, and she encouraged me to submit more of my fiction, shared a website where one can research different periodicals, urged me to find an agent for this collection of days of grieving, and to query magazine editors about publishing a section of the whole chronicle. On our way out of the coffee shop, we ran into Tracey, another writer, whom I was happy to introduce to Meghan and who may have hooked Meghan up with a much needed tutoring gig. By the end of the morning, I felt very invigorated, like there had been all this good writing karma floating around with people put in my way so that connections could happen. I love this sort of flow: win, win, win, everywhere, and I can't help but feel Maggie nudging me along: go on, get back to it, put it out there, be a writer.

Meg Tipper

September 10

Dragging

I thought about Stephen all day and then forgot to call him for his birthday. That was symbolic of my state of mind, not really there, absorbed in myself. I have been fighting to keep above the sadness, and it twists up my mind and sucks my energy. What little I have done today felt like a show I was putting on: Meg acting like she is living her life.

September 11

Tax Refund

About a month ago, Maggie received notification from the IRS that because she had not cashed her 2007 refund check, and because the check was only valid for one year, they would be issuing her another. One part of me was delighted: it was vintage Maggie to space out on cashing her check or, even more likely, to lose it. This also meant that we would have an additional $309.00 to put into her fund. Another part of me, the part that had to spend hours on the phone, plowing through the IRS red tape, was annoyed at Maggie for being irresponsible about her money. What piled on top of the annoyance was the thought that it was good Maggie died before she really had to function in the world as a responsible adult. I was immediately dismayed and horrified by this thought, aware of how selfish, petty, and really insane it was.

September 12

Fights

Jim and I had a fight, a silly small thing, as they usually are, but with a bigger issue behind it, as is also usually the case. I hate fights. Maggie and I used to fight a lot, and I don't want to forget that fact in the way I recreate her and our relationship in my mind. We were both very opinionated, smart, and articulate, and we could get into it, big time.

September 13

The Story

Since my talk with Meghan last week, I have been thinking more about the marketability of these daily entries, this story of grieving Maggie. What has been troubling me is that this story begins with the climax, boom. Completely unexpectedly, with no development, we are all launched into this maelstrom of a world turned upside down. I don't even get to establish the world as it was, except in retrospect. Then, all the rest is *dénouement*, the slow, daily winding out of consequences, sometimes *ad nauseum*. And, perhaps most dissatisfying for a potential reader, whenever I choose to end this, (and I have always had in my mind that it would be one year of days), there will be no neat conclusion, no comforting feeling that we have brought the story to a close. Who would want to live 365 days of that story? And still, I write, because it is more than something to publish; it is something positive and generative and, to the best of my ability, true, something to create out of the destruction of one of the most beautiful and treasured parts of my life, something that might help someone else.

September 14

Sadness

The weather has been unseasonably cool since Jim and I have been back from Bonaire. We have been sleeping under quilts, wearing layers. It is dark when I get up to go to my meeting in the morning, and all day long the sun is lower in the sky. All my life I have fought sadness, especially in the fall. About six years ago, when I finally slipped into full-blown depression over everything that happened with Bill, I got clear about what I had been up against. I guess part of me always knew that there was a deep and frighteningly dark place where I did not want to live.

Since then, I have taken a low-dose anti-depressant, which usually is very effective in keeping my symptoms under control. However, for the last few weeks, I have been working really hard against the pull down; it is like swimming against a current, discouraging and exhausting. It is hard work, but also confusing, because I have every right to be sad. I am in mourning; I am missing my daughter. I need to let myself grieve. And so there is this see-saw between pushing up to stay positive, grateful, focused on others, productive, and healthy, and letting myself sink into the natural cycles of mourning, feeling the sadness and letting it move through without resistance.

September 15

Cold Crops

For the first time in my life, I am planting cold crops. Normally, by the end of the summer, I am ready to put the garden to bed, but this year I have eagerly bought seeds, rearranged weed guard and hoses to create more rows where the big viney plants were growing all summer, and, today, I have planted: spinach, lettuce, radishes, turnips, boc choy, kale, and chard. I still have onions and garlic left to do. There is pretty much nothing more therapeutic for me than having my hands in the dirt and tending to growing things. The work is a kind of meditation, and I often achieve a very quiet mind. Today, I relished this perfect, clear, sunny, warm afternoon in my garden, serenaded by crickets, attended by butterflies.

September 16

Acceptance

In Dennis Lehane's novel, *Mystic River*, the morning after his daughter's burial following her brutal murder, Jimmy Marcus awakes, finds he has slept late, and replies in answer to his neighbor's concerned question, "'You okay?' 'Yeah,' Jimmy said, and it surprised him to realize that, in fact, he did feel okay. He still carried Katie in him like a second stricken and angry heart that would never, he was certain, stop beating its mad beat. He had no illusions about that. The grief was a constant now, more a part of him than a limb. But somehow during his long sleep, he'd gained an elemental acceptance of it. There it was, part of him, and he could deal with it on those terms. And so, under the circumstances, he felt far better than he would have expected. 'I'm . . . all right'" (391).

This passage did not ring true to me. Not that everyone whose child dies suddenly will grieve in the same way that I am, but somehow I don't see any parent able to wrap his or her head around anything like acceptance of the grief in just a few days. To me, the very fact of my child's death, of the loss, was not even real then, let alone the nature and extent of the grief. And now, over ten months in, I am nowhere near acceptance. I try to observe the process and to wrestle it into words, but I am still often drowning in all that feels alien and completely unacceptable.

September 17

Small Talk

For my birthday, Jim and I have traveled to Maine, one of my favorite places in the world. We are staying at the Inn at Bath, guests of my old high school friend Elizabeth Knowlton, with an upgrade to a room with a fireplace and hot tub, thanks to my dear old friend Susan McChesney, who lives nearby. There are interesting fellow travelers at the Inn to meet and chat with. This morning at breakfast, talk turned to home towns, travel, professions, and, inevitably, children. I listened to people speak of their grown sons and daughters and felt pleased and proud to have Stephen and Ira and Zeke to crow about, but I tucked Maggie into my heart, unable to open that pain up in front of strangers.

I felt bewildered by my first encounters with Susan in many years. Clearly she was extending her heart to me: the room at the Inn, a birthday cake, a cancelled appointment so that we could spend more time together, the gift of a print of one of her beautiful drawings, but never in the time we spent together did she speak of Maggie. I am sure it was a matter of no words seeming like the right thing to say. With Elizabeth, it was much the same: warmth, big hugs, lots of attention, but the subject of Maggie came out indirectly and a ways into our time together. In telling me a story of a loss in her own family, Elizabeth said, "As you well know, no parent should have to bury a child," and she began to cry.

Maybe it's different for other grieving parents, but for me, there is never a wrong time or way to open to my grief. Speaking of Maggie never makes me more sad.

September 18

The Ghana Quilt

Maggie returned from her semester in Ghana with a large piece of fabric made from big sections of traditional African fabric sewn together. She told me that she wanted to make a quilt, so we worked on resewing sections to make the piece more flat. We chose a fabric for backing and cut the batting. Mags took everything with her out to L. A., intending to finish the quilt over the summer while she was working for the Enterprise Foundation. However, there were always more fun things to do than sew, so when I went out to be with her for Thanksgiving of her senior year, I promised that we would finish the quilt together. I brought the embroidery thread for tying, and Maggie scrubbed the floor of the notoriously filthy "Ranch" where she lived, mostly with guys. I slept at a nearby hotel, but spent a lot of the wonderful long weekend squatting on top of the quilt on Maggie's living room floor, stitching through the layers and tying knots. My thighs ached for a week afterwards! I brought the quilt back home, finished the edges on my machine, and mailed it back to Maggie. It was bright and colorful and cheerful and it reminded her of Ghana and me of her.

After Maggie died, I gave Stephen this quilt. It is on

his bed and last night, Jim and I slept under it. I wept as I pulled it around us: missing Maggie, remembering making it, and thinking about how precious Jim and Stephen are to me. This morning, after I made the bed and smoothed the quilt, I tightened some of the knots.

September 19

Boston Revisited

In the summer of '08, I saw that Grace Potter and the Nocturnals would be playing in Boston around my birthday, so I got three tickets and told Stephen and Maggie that we would go together. Mags said, "Mom, I have no idea where I'll be then," and I said, "Don't worry, wherever you are, I'll get you there." Something made me feel how important it would be for us to have that time together.

Now, almost exactly a year later, Jim and I have stopped in Boston for a long weekend before heading home from Maine. It is eerie and emotional walking past the restaurant in Porter Square where Maggie and I propped our suitcases against the railing and ate lunch outside, seeing the coffee shop we ducked into to get out of the rain, opening a cabinet in Stephen's kitchen and finding the Chrystal Light we bought because Maggie was on that strict ketogenic diet. It is so surreal to remember all that and to realize—that was it. That was the last time Maggie and I would come visit Stephen, that was the last trip she and I would take together. And it is so hard to hold these conflicting feelings: gratitude for that time and anger and sorrow for the future pleasures that were stolen from us.

September 20

The Better Child to Die

Today I had another totally insane thought. Stephen's car battery died and Jim helped him replace it. As I sat on the curb and watched them bent together over the battery, I thought: *Jim is so good with Stephen; he gets boys. If I had to lose a child, it was good that it was Maggie, because it's easier for Jim to have a good relationship with Stephen. In fact,* I thought, *it's probably easier for me to have a good relationship with Stephen; mother-daughter relationships are so intense. Plus Maggie was still carrying baggage from the divorce, and she wouldn't really let herself warm up to Jim. So, all in all, Maggie was the better child to die.*

It is so embarrassing, horrifying really, to admit having thoughts like these, but there they are.

September 21

Stand Up Comedy

Tonight Jim and I saw Margaret Cho perform. She is really raunchy, and we laughed until we cried. The last time I saw a stand-up comedian live was when Bill and I went with Maggie in L.A. to see Bob Saget. I had no idea Saget was a comedian; I was familiar with him only as Danny Tanner on *Full House* and as the host of *America's Funniest Home Videos*. In those two very wholesome roles, he is clean cut, the perfect family man. On stage though, Saget's language is vulgar, his subject matter sick and oh, yes, he is very funny! But it is the sort of humor I felt embarrassed to laugh at in front of my eighteen year old daughter. Not that Maggie was in any way protected or prudish, just that there were some things I preferred she not know I thought were funny! Maggie loved Saget, and she would have loved Margaret Cho. I missed her, but it was wildly good to laugh that hard.

September 22

Gifts

I have created a new post on Maggie's Facebook page to announce the first gifts made from the Maggie Feiss Fund. When Bill, Stephen and I met with Tom Wilcox of the BCF, we decided to focus our initial efforts on three of the many causes Maggie worked for and believed in. We would give our largest gift of ten thousand dollars to help improve public transportation in Baltimore; another grant would become a scholarship to enable a promising young person from Baltimore to attend college, and one would go to the Living Classrooms Foundation where Maggie was due to begin working on November 3, the day after she died. In addition, for us, we made a large gift to CURE, Citizens United for Research in Epilepsy, in hopes that Maggie's Fund will be a part of finding a cure and stopping the debilitation and sometimes death that can result from uncontrolled seizures. We are profoundly grateful to everyone who contributed to the Fund for enabling us to make these gifts on Maggie's behalf. We hope that through further donations and through fund-raising projects, we will be able to grow the Fund and continue to make a difference in Baltimore and in the world.

September 23

Josie

About a week ago, I received a mass email from an old friend with whom I went to summer camp, alerting me to watch the *Today Show* on Monday morning as another campmate, Sorrel King, would be talking about her book, *Josie's Story*, about her daughter's death and about Sorrel's fight against medical error. Josie King died because of mistakes made in her care at Johns Hopkins Hospital. I wasn't able to watch the show, but I reserved the book at the library and picked it up yesterday morning and finished it in a day. King writes well, and this seems to be the only sort of book I want to read about grief: other people's stories.

The road to Josie's death was torturous: a terrible accident which resulted in severe burns over 60% of her body, over two weeks in the hospital as she slowly improved, and then a sudden crash, ending with Josie having a heart attack and finally being removed from life support. I felt grateful that our experience was different, that we were spared all of that pain and shot straight to the core of it: Maggie was dead. However, the aftermath of our children's deaths was entirely familiar: the shock, the inability to function, the desire to die, the anger. As I read, I envied King her white hot anger at Johns Hopkins Hospital; it seemed a luxury to have a big institution on which to place the blame, against which to rail. And I envied her crusade as a patient safety advocate, something she can now dive into and see the good that has come from Josie's death. I also envied her her three young children who still need her, who create sound and activity and energy in her life, who make a real family, who are siblings for each other. And I even envied her her pregnancy, the chance to bring a new life to the world once again, to feel hope and new love alongside the grief.

For all that I envied Sorrel King as I read her story, my strongest feeling was that I wanted to meet her. I wanted to talk with her about mourning our daughters, about writing a book and getting it published. She lives in my town, we shared a summer camp experience, and now we share that haunting emptiness that lives inside every parent who has lost a child. I will call.

September 24

Letting Go

This morning while I was saying my prayers, it occurred to me that I have never given my grief to my higher power. I have asked for help, over and over again, but I have never, in almost eleven months, asked for this grieving to be removed. And immediately, right behind that thought was the clutch, the realization that I am not ready to give up my grief. My grief is my post-death umbilical cord to Maggie. But now, understanding that I have a choice, that one day at a time, when I am ready, I can give this pain to my God, I feel a shift.

Since Maggie died, the grief has settled into me like a heavy ball of dough, which I have kneaded, let rise, punched down, watched rise again, and punched, and kneaded, and this cycle could go on forever. But the day is coming when it will be time to bake the bread, and the dough will change into something beautiful and delicious and life sustaining. The oven will cool, and Maggie will be there, nourishing me, forever.

September 25

Dahlias

I visited with Mom and she had a perfect dahlia blossom sitting in a bowl of water on her coffee table. "Oh, dahlias," I sighed, "they remind me of Maggie." "We must go see them," Mom said.

Last year at this time, with Maggie home and at loose ends, she spent more time with her grandmother than she had in years. One of the things they did on her visits to Mom's retirement community was to go look at the dahlias in the community garden. Maggie had come to love the exotic dahlias grown by the grandmother of a family she babysat for, and there was something about the huge blossoms with their complex petals and splashy colors that spoke to her. She was not especially a flower person, but she loved dahlias.

So Mom and I walked to the garden in the waning light of a beautiful fall afternoon and cupped the blossoms in our hands, weighing their symmetrical beauty.

September 26

Stages of Grief

Jim and I watched the episode of the TV show *Grey's Anatomy* in which George dies, which tore us up because we love George. The theme was grief. At the end, the camera froze on faces of the main characters as they went about their lives and the voice over explained the "stages of grief" one hears and reads about.

I know that in 1969, when *On Death and Dying* was published, there was little awareness or discussion of death and dying. The psychiatrist Elizabeth Kubler Ross made an enormous contribution in observing patients with terminal illnesses and giving people both in and outside the medical profession a framework for understanding, and she was quick to caution that her model of "stages" was not a process that necessarily would unfold in a systematic way. However, her theory has been applied outside the narrow context from which she formulated it, and many, the popular media perhaps first among them, now seem to appropriate the model for all sorts of loss and to expect that there will be a logical progression through the stages. And, of course, our culture being what it is, there also seems to be a popular expectation that one should move from stage to stage quickly and efficiently, as though there were a grief assembly line.

I can lie in bed in the morning and flip through every "stage" almost simultaneously, almost as though my mind wants to torture me with the full range of everything grief can throw at me. Sometimes I can pray my way through and feel some relief; sometimes I just have to force myself out of bed.

September 27

Trudge

Grieving is a trudge. Sometimes it weighs so heavily, I feel like I can't breathe, can't move.

There is a line at the conclusion of the opening section of the book *Alcoholics Anonymous*: "you will surely meet some of us as you trudge the Road of Happy Destiny" (164). There is much in that line: the assurance of the company of others on the road, people who understand and provide support along the journey, the acknowledgment that the walk will be a trudge, long and arduous, but also that the road itself is a happy end. I have never before understood the first part of that line so well. I am less attuned to the Road of Happy Destiny. I have known and felt that way of traveling as a recovering person, happy in the serenity and fulfillment of a life of service in recovery. I have far less confidence that trudging the road of grief can be anything other than this smothering, debilitating weight. And yet, I walk.

September 28

24 Hours

Jim and I have been watching the first season of the television series *24* on video. It is riveting and we can become addicted, promising each other that we will watch only one more and then compelled by the end of the episode to keep going to the next. I love the premise, a minute by minute playing out of one 24-hour day.

Perhaps not coincidentally, I was at a meeting last week, and I confessed to a friend that I was having a hard time fighting depression. She asked, "Is it seasonal?" and I said, yes, probably partially, but also that I suspected that coming up to the anniversary of Maggie's death was part of it. We talked about how my memories of the waning days of Maggie's life are so strong, that there is that special poignancy of remembering them while at the same time knowing the future, and that during anniversaries, there is the inevitable tension between reflection and staying in the present. Not only was it very helpful to talk, but my friend also said, "Perhaps this will help," and she took out a little bag from her pocketbook from which she removed a recovery medallion, one of the discs we give to people to mark recovery time. This one said: 24 hours. When she pressed it into my hand, it was cold, but the metal quickly warmed, and I held it loosely throughout the meeting, then slipped it into my pocket.

September 29

Writing

I awoke and could not go back to sleep, which happens from time to time. I lie awake for no more than an hour and then I get up and stay up until I get sleepy or until morning. Last night, I listened to a Fresh Air interview with poet Kathleen Bonanno, whose book, *Slamming Open the Door*, chronicles the aftermath of her daughter's murder. Bonanno is a high school English teacher, a Unitarian Universalist, and a fine writer. I felt a cord of intimate connection as I listened, partially because Terry Gross is such a good interviewer and mostly because Bonanno is so honest, both in the interview and especially in her poems.

Bonanno spoke some about her writing; two things stuck out. First was the idea that she came to realize that she was teaching in some of the poems: having found herself the actor in an unimaginable drama, she felt compelled to teach the lines and the script to the next actor to play the part of "mother of the murdered daughter." This might sound strange to someone who has not walked through it, but I have felt the same impulse in these writings, wanting others who mourn to know they are not alone, to know that they will survive and also wanting to teach about Maggie and the way she lived so abundantly. Bonanno also mentions that she was compelled to write these poems because "her [Leidy's] death stood in the way of my other writing." In one poem, entitled "Death Barged In," she concludes, "Even as I sit here, / he stands behind me / clamping two / colossal hands / on my shoulders / and bends down / and whispers to my neck: / From now on, / you write about me." I know this voice. Sometimes, there is nothing else but the death.

September 30

Panic

On the heels of the "something you can sink your teeth into" conversation I had with Jim in Bonaire at the beginning of September, I came home and set up an appointment to talk with Tom Wilcox of the Baltimore Community Foundation. I like and admire and respect Tom so much, and I feel so much hope for Baltimore when I am around him. In fact, I feel better about everything. I met with him today and shared my idea that perhaps I could be of some service to BCF, that I might be ready to give a little more of myself. That offer felt good, and Tom was very receptive and supportive. Then we began to do some brainstorming about how I might help. Honestly, every idea Tom came up with filled me with dread. I could muster some confidence in speaking generally of the kinds of things I like to do and what I'm good at, but when we imagined me into specific situations, I just felt scared and incompetent. Fortunately, I know Tom well enough and feel comfortable enough with him that I could be honest about all that. I even cried. I finally suggested that he put me to work stuffing envelopes, since I'm a Virgo and do really neat, sharp folds. We did have some smiles over that and over discovering that our birthdays are on the same day.

Tom was so gracious; he said he would find a place for me in the "family." At home, Jim and I laughed about poor Tom having to go back to the office and roll his eyes with his colleagues about another crazy relation whom BCF needs to take care of. Bless him.

October 1

Drama

I had a voice mail on my phone from a friend who is sad that I can't be more present for her right now. She said that she was not used to feeling like she is being a burden to me. She said she wondered if it were because of the loss I'm coping with. I feel badly that I have hurt her feelings, but that she even has to ask shows me how little I have been able to convey to her honestly about the ways in which grief occupies my mind and heart, about how much work it is on some days just to live life in the simplest ways.

October 2

The Red Bug

Last night I dreamt of seeing a small red bug on a couch, which I brushed onto the floor and then squished with my foot. But when I took my shoe away and looked, the bug was not dead, a little smashed, but still wiggling. So I stepped on it again, and this time pressed down harder and ground my shoe in a little, but still, it was alive, and it was growing stronger and bigger. There was nothing sinister about the bug; I never thought it was going to harm me, I just wanted to kill it because it didn't belong in my house. However, no matter how hard I tried, I couldn't kill it. I finally was on the floor, wrestling with it; it was as large as I was. I had my arms around it and with leverage, I was trying to snap its neck, but I wasn't strong enough to overcome its resistance. I was straining to the point of total exhaustion; that is all I remember.

Part of me wonders if I am supposed to get help killing the bug. But another part knows that the true answer lies in accepting the red bug on my couch, in knowing that we can both sit there in peace and that it is only in trying to kill it that it grows and overpowers me.

It is eleven months since Maggie died, and this big red bug ain't going anywhere soon.

October 3

Rabbit Hole

Mom warned me about this play: "It is hard for anyone, even if they haven't lost a child." As Jim and I were driving to the Everyman Theatre to see it, I said, "I'm apprehensive about this," to which Jim replied, "Yeah, maybe we should just go get hot fudge sundaes." But we already had our tickets and part of me wanted to see the play.

David Lindsay-Abaire's title comes from the idea of a Lewis Carroll world in which everything is upside down, out of proportion, and kind of crazy. His characters are all dealing in their own ways both with their grief in the aftermath of the tragic accident that killed their son/nephew/grandson and with their own limitations as human beings, trying to carry on with already complicated and imperfect relationships.

The intensity of the emotion was cut by wonderfully funny moments, yes moments in which the characters can laugh at themselves and each other, but more frequently moments in which we, the audience, can see humor that is even more poignant because the characters can't see it. I came away not wracked as I had expected to be, but rather comforted. Everyone else had been forced to live in and understand my world for a little while. They were wracked and I was unscathed. How could Lindsay-Abaire's *Rabbit Hole* have done otherwise? I was already in it.

October 4

Sisters

Dee's daughter got married yesterday. I have known Dani since she was a baby and have listened to Dee talk for a year about the wedding plans at our monthly bridge games. Of course, I wanted to be there, but I knew it would be a difficult night. Most of the really emotional moments though were somehow for Bill: watching Steve walk his daughter down the aisle, both of them beaming, full of joy and love, and then the father-daughter dance, playful and intimate. It wasn't until all of Dani's sorority sisters gathered around her for a dance that I really sobbed for myself. There was something about the joy of that sisterhood that made me think about how Maggie would be missing from the circles of her friends when they get married and how the only time her friends will all have gathered for her was at her funeral. On the other hand, there I was, flanked all night by two of my best girlfriends who were taking such good care of me. As I had that cry, I took Kathy's hand and rested my head on her shoulder.

October 5

Grief Blogs

At the wedding, I talked to a poet and teacher whom I have not seen in years. She asked what I have been writing and I told her about Maggie's death and about this project. In turn, she told me about her friend and fellow writer, Christine Higgins, who lost her sixteen year old daughter, her only child, in a car accident in June and about the blog site that she has created: *The Green Door: Ushering Grief.* I looked it up when I got home and read many of her entries. Higgins writes well, and I was touched by the similarities between us: another mother trying to keep her head above water by writing.

Then I made the mistake of googling "grief blogs" and the search turned up over four million hits. I went to several sites and concluded that there is a lot of strange, often schlocky, often religious, often pop psychological stuff out there. I also concluded that grief is big business. I have returned to Higgins' blog with renewed appreciation for someone who feels more like a kindred spirit than the authors of other sites I visited.

October 6

Betsey Johnson Dress

For Dani's fancy Saturday night wedding, I wore a gorgeous dress that Maggie found for me. Bill and I were in L.A. for parents' weekend Maggie's sophomore year, and Mags and I went shopping in Melrose, an area Maggie had found with upscale thrift stores and other funky shops. We had so much fun that day; I got two things that I still have, and I love to wear them both. Mags pulled this dress off the rack and exclaimed, "Mom, this is a Betsey Johnson! It's fabulous!" Of course, being hopelessly NOT into fashion, I had no idea who the designer was, but I did love the dress, a slinky cut-velvet in black, maroon, and olive green. The bottom is uneven, and both Maggie and I thought it would be great for dancing. I tried it on, and it fit me perfectly. Though it was expensive for a used dress, Maggie insisted that it was made for me, a great deal, and that I must buy it. I felt beautiful and sexy on Saturday night, and I know Maggie was proud of me for going out and dancing and having a good time at Dani's wedding in my Betsey Johnson dress.

October 7

Rejection & Possibility

Years ago I decided that I would stop sending my writing out for publication. I have a fragile sense of myself as a writer and less need for public acclaim than I have for the freedom to write comfortably. Still, I was seduced recently by my friend's asking for a manuscript. His rejection, which came a week ago by email, was debilitating. All the old "why bother" crap came crashing down. Still, I can see the rejection now as a gift, because I was able to know for sure that I have neither the energy nor the fortitude to withstand any rejections of this manuscript. These words, wrung from my heart, will not be marketed. This day by day testimony to the process and simple fact of surviving Maggie's death, this creation out of the destruction of my life as I knew it, will be mine to bring to light.

One of the ways I am growing through my grieving has been to accept my limitations. Because my energy is low and my life feels so heavy, instead of bullying my way through resistance, I have had to learn to look for other paths that are beckoning. And so, I talked yesterday with my long-time writing and teaching colleague, Lucy Hoopes, about publishing options. I learned a lot, and felt grateful to have a friend in the business. She showed me books that had been self published and suggested that I also look into Apprentice House at Loyola University, which gives students an opportunity to learn the business of publishing by working with real authors and their manuscripts. This option appeals to me on many levels and I am excited to explore it. Maybe publishing this book will be the thing that I am meant to sink my teeth into.

October 8

The Four of Us

I went through some of Mom's photographs last week in order to make some cards for her, and I found one that she took last November 7. It was an afternoon when my brothers, Mom and I had gathered for lunch together and Mom suggested a picture. I remember feeling like that was the last thing I wanted to do, but my brothers literally gathered me up: Bill with his hand on my heart, Kendal's hand on my shoulder and Charlie with his head pressed against mine. We all looked intently at Mom through the camera lens, and there is the most amazing combination of pain and love in those eyes. When I saw the picture, it was a searing reminder, capturing as it does the support I received from my brothers and the loss all of us were suffering. I am glad to have that picture, which, as far as I know, is the only one from those terrible days.

Meg Tipper

October 9

Shower the People You Love With Love

Last week was so hard. I felt defeated, exhausted, and yes, scared, terrified of facing day after day of this pain. I felt like I couldn't breathe, like there was no crack in the heavy sadness. Then I had the red bug dream, and I was asked to lead a twelve step recovery meeting, I had some good conversations with friends, my prayers deepened, and this morning I awakened with an awareness of the refrain of the James Taylor song in my mind: "Shower the people you love with love." It is one of the songs on my Maggie playlist, added after one of my visits to Florida this past winter to be with Kendal and Janet. We watched a James Taylor live video on which he played that song, and we all welled up and met each others' tearful eyes, knowing that we each were holding some of the gifts of Maggie's death: appreciating still having the people we love in our lives, feeling how being able to love Maggie and each other keeps her alive, feeling how she is still loving us.

And as I have gone through my day, I have felt soft and loving and appreciative and connected and not scared.

October 10

White Iris & Purple Crocuses

Sometime in early September, I noticed that there was one white iris blooming in my flower bed along the back of the garage. I thought it was strange. Now, there are purple crocuses up everywhere, laying themselves open in the waning mid-day fall sun and then tightening up against the evening chill, just as they do in March. And this too is strange, but they make me smile. Anytime something in nature grabs my attention, I imagine it is Maggie finding a way to reach me.

Standing at the Edge

October 11

Launching

When the children were young, Bill and I decided that we would get a family portrait painted. However, we did not want anything traditional; we had in mind something that would be visually appealing as a painting but which would capture our family. We found a local artist, Betty Bowman, who was willing to work with us, and she spent a beautiful fall afternoon in our back yard, taking pictures while we played with the dogs, piled onto the hammock, and raked leaves into piles for the kids to jump into or run through. The painting is lovely, with Bill and Stephen raking and me pushing the hammock, launching Maggie, who is flying into a leaf pile, arms akimbo, her face alight, her hair wild. How amazing that, perhaps close to twenty years later, it was fall and Maggie went flying off. And I will spend the rest of my life working to let her go!

Recently I came across a poem which I wrote at a poetry workshop, years ago. Strange how everything cycles:

Falling Leaves

Taste like burnt toast
a penny under the tongue
stale bread or
corn flakes

Smell like fire
foam on the shore
grocery bags or
dirt raked

Sound like looking
through paper
a whisper or
a sigh

Feel like sinking
rusting cars
piling up problems or
wanting to die

Look like acrobats
dealing cards
what we don't know and
letting go

October 12

Company Coming

A week from today Jim's step mother and step sister from Japan are coming to visit us for ten days. It was just under a year ago that we made our trip to Japan to see them, our last travels before Maggie died. They are gracious, generous, fun, and loving people, and I look forward to their company. Still, I am unsure about having house guests in the weeks leading up to the anniversary. On the one hand, Mitsuko and Sumiko's visit will be a good distraction, and we will be busy, but I will have to be sure to protect my quiet and private times: my writing, my yoga, prayer, and meditation, my meetings, all the things I do to help me stay afloat.

October 13

Why?

I talked with Bill yesterday for the first time in ages. Without any explicit agreement, we had given each other some space, which I think was helpful. I know that Bill has struggled ever since Maggie died with the question, why? and with a sense of his own responsibility for her death. I have been blessed not to. Perhaps because of my faith and my experiences in recovery, I have become more comfortable with the inexplicable and I know that much happens for which no one is responsible.

Coincidentally, Anu Garg's A.Word.A.Day for October 13, 2009 is *vis major*. Garg defines it as, "noun: An unavoidable disruptive event (such as an earthquake) that none of the parties is responsible for, which may exempt them from the obligations of a contract. Natural instances of vis major are also called acts of God. ETYMOLOGY: From Latin vis major, literally, greater force."

October 14

Surrogate Daughter

My friend Stephanie is getting married at the end of October. She is just a little older than Maggie, and she knows that she's one of my surrogate daughters. Stephanie has been having a rocky time with her own mother lately and needed to have someone accompany her for a fitting of her wedding dress. I offered and she took me up on it.

I sat on the couch at the seamstress; Stephanie stood in front of the three-way mirror while Isabel cut the crinoline and the underskirt, pinned the hem and tacked the bustle. I had brought the necklace that Bill gave me for a wedding present, because Stephanie had told me that she was looking for a delicate vintage necklace to wear. I put it around her neck and said, "Something borrowed," as I fastened it. I stood looking at her as she took in her reflection. "It's perfect," she said, touching the thin, gold chain. "Thank you." I just buried my head into her hair; I couldn't speak.

Later she wrote me an email, "I am so glad that you could be there with me today. I know this is not how either of us imagined doing something like this." No, it's not, but it was a sweet gift, and I'll take it. Maggie had loads of surrogates: The Strauss family was her surrogate family when hers was falling apart; Luke and Charlie were her surrogate younger brothers. It took a village to provide that girl with all the love and attention she needed! Now I need to learn from her: to collect my surrogate daughters, to share in their lives, and to allow them to love me.

October 15

French

I have returned to my French class and I love it. We laugh, we practice, none of us is very good, but we try hard and are very supportive of one another, we have fun. Sometimes I even forget that I am in mourning.

I still have my notes and papers from my class last fall, and when I was organizing my notebook, I found homework in which I had written the following: J'ai deux enfants, mon âiné, Stephen, est professeur de mathématiques à Boston. Ma fille, Maggie, a fini ses études universitaires; maintenant elle habite à Baltimore. Ma fille est un très bon compagnon de voyage, avec un grand esprit d'aventure...

How cavalierly I had written those words last fall, confident in both my children's solid presence in my life! Now, I read one of the last sentences in that same homework and think how much more true it is today than when I wrote it a year ago: Je crois que le secret d'être joyeux est d'embrasser toutes les activités quotidiennes.

October 16

The Big Adventure

Maggie loved to travel. She had planned to take off after graduating from college to do a round the world trip. As her seizures became progressively worse, she clearly could not travel alone but was always hoping that after her friends Stephanie, whom she called Seb, and Amy graduated in 2009, the three of them would take off for the big adventure.

Seb contacted me recently to tell me that she will be leaving Sunday for Thailand. She has a job teaching English and has bought a one-way ticket! I anticipated a plan of this kind and have spoken with Bill and Stephen to get their blessing: we want Seb to take some of Maggie's ashes with her.

I met Seb yesterday afternoon for coffee. It was a dreary, cold, rainy day, and in the pocket of my raincoat, I carried some of Maggie's ashes. Ever practical, the best means of transportation, light and flexible and sealable: a plastic bag. Maggie in a baggie. We had a good laugh, and Seb promised to set her free from a mountain top in Thailand.

October 17

Nightmare

A few days ago, I was talking to Bill about what he might want to do around the anniversary. He said, "What I really want to do is just wake up and find that this nightmare is over."

This past weekend, Jim and I participated in festivities for his 40th high school reunion—the class of 1969. I knew no one there other than Jim, whom they all call Jamie, so even he seemed a bit strange to me, a different name and sense of himself among these old friends. Inevitably people asked me about my children, and having decided ahead of time that I was not going to be the mother of a dead girl, I smiled and told people about my two wonderful children, a little about their lives. It was fine and light and, I think, appropriate. And, it was kind of fun, for awhile, to pretend.

On the other hand, it was not real. It was the same feeling that I had when I thought about Bill's wish. As terrible, horrifying, and devastating as Maggie's death has been, it happened. And it has woven itself into my life and into who I am. Her death is as much a part of me now as her life is.

October 18

News

I have been rereading some of these entries, and I realize how disconnected from the world they are. There are precious few moments in the past year when my awareness has reached much beyond the borders of a very contained sphere. I have never been a news junkie, but I have always liked to be informed about what's going on. I am a long time NPR listener, and I used to love to read *The Sun* before it became an embarrassment. However, for many months after Maggie died, I could not listen to or read the news. I had no space in my mind or heart for drama or controversy, my inner landscape was so vast and terrifying, it was all I could navigate. For many months, I couldn't stand anything but silence in the car. Even music drained me. Even now, more often than not, when I turn on the news, I end up turning it off; it is just more than I can take in. I have resorted to *New York Times* headlines in my email. It is shameful.

October 19

The Fullness of Fall

It is getting harder and harder to forget that fall is here and that fall is the season in which Maggie died. She is everywhere: the crispness of the air, the red edges of the leaves, pumpkin pie, Halloween decorations, thinking about costumes, wood smoke. I am having such a strange relationship with all of it, loving the season but also dreading this inexorable march to the anniversary of her death.

As I walked in the woods this morning, I drank in the trees backlit by the rising sun, the cold water of the lake foggy as the sun hit it, the loamy smells of the forest, the geese calling. I felt how precious it is to be in this body, full in my life. I also felt that Maggie's spirit is slipping away from remembering sensation, that physical embodiment is losing its pull for her. I have a terrible time putting words to this, but it was a strong feeling.

Standing at the Edge

October 20

Permission to Die

Last fall, my dear old friend Sarah helped me survive the wedding weekend in Chapel Hill, just a few weeks after Maggie died. Now, this fall, she has just walked through her step-mother's passing. Vera had been ill for awhile; she had not eaten in a month, had not had liquids in nine days. The hospice nurses were giving her morphine and told Sarah and her father to summon the family; the end was near. Vera lived for four more days.

When I told this story to Mom, she said, "People need permission to die. Sometimes they are holding on for someone or something." I said, "Yes, and some people die without our permission."

Tonight, when I grabbed some quiet time outside as the sky darkened, the crescent moon glowed, and the bats swooped after insects, I got twisted up in thinking about Maggie's actual death. I have spent very little time doing that—it is a land of the unknown, fraught with potential for torturing myself. But I did have this feeling that Maggie had given herself permission to die, to stop fighting her disease. I have to believe that it was a peaceful passing.

October 21

L.A.

Jim, Mom, and I watched the PBS recording of Gustavo Dudamel's inaugural concert in his new position as music director of the L. A. Philharmonic. The man is electric with his big energy, and he chose a brave work for his opening: a premier of John Adams' new piece, a meditation on Los Angeles entitled "City Noir." I kept thinking how much Maggie would have loved all of it: this magnetic, young (28!) Venezuelan conductor, this vibrant and innovative piece of music about the city she called home for four years, the exuberance of the young and ethnically diverse crowd outside the Disney Concert Hall. Surely I would have called to check that she was watching. Surely we would have talked about a new age in classical music.

October 22

Alive in His Mind

Recently Maggie received a message on her Facebook wall from one of her friends in Ghana: "Hey, Maggie, waz up? Long time since I heard from you." Kwame had not read her page carefully and, of course, would have had no other way to learn of her death. I couldn't bring myself to write to him. I loved the idea that for Kwame, Maggie was still alive, not the kind of alive we all do to keep her close, but really, truly alive.

October 23

Lost Children

At a meeting today, a mother spoke about how she was so irresponsible at the end stages of her drinking that her ex husband got sole custody of her children and that now they are estranged. Her voice was full of pain as she spoke about having "lost" her children. Part of me screamed inside: "but they are still alive!" Another part of me cried with her, unable to imagine the horror of feeling responsible for actions that caused her children to be taken away. At least my loss is through no fault of my own. It is more permanent, but perhaps more kind.

October 24

Other Mothers

I watch other mothers, particularly mothers and their daughters. I am a voracious voyeur and I take in their relationships, jealous even of their fights. At the same time, I am more keenly aware of myself as a daughter, so grateful that my mother is alive and that I have more time, now that I am retired, to be a loving and attentive daughter.

October 25

Another Funeral

Yesterday I attended the funeral of the brother of my former sister-in-law, Cathy. Jeff Roberts was young; he died of brain cancer after a long fight. I had steeled myself for the funeral and did not find it difficult, I felt for Cathy, but the grief of the loss did not touch me personally. I didn't cry. I remember thinking that I was so glad that both Jeff's parents were dead so that they would not have to suffer this death.

I dashed to the car after the service, unable to face the small talk outside the church. There, I sat and watched people walking to their cars, watched the yellow leaves tumbling, and I returned a phone call to Janet, with whom I had been playing phone tag for almost a week. With no children of their own, Janet and Kendal had a special bond with Maggie, and Maggie could talk to Janet about things she could not bring to other people. I knew this approaching anniversary would be weighing on her.

I finally found both Kendal and Janet at home and we had a good long talk. Janet told me that she had desperately wanted to tell me about her dream. "You know, in all this time, I have not dreamed of Maggie. It was killing me. Every night, I would pray to her to come to me. And then, finally, I had this crazy dream with people I hardly know in it, but Maggie was there, and she gave me a big hug and said, 'It is so good to hug you.' And that was it. But I was so happy in the dream and still so happy when I woke up and all the way to work." Of course, we were both weeping as Janet related the dream to me. I had had no idea that I needed to cry. But it was good, the tears brought me back into myself, and I was able to go to the reception and connect with people, look into their eyes, be there.

October 26

Is This Your Daughter?

Jim's step mother and I have almost no common language between us, but we are very fond of each other. I had sensed that Mitsuko wanted to connect with me around Maggie's death, but that finding the vehicle was a challenge. The room Mitsuko is staying in is the place where I do yoga, meditate, and where I have a little shrine with pictures of Maggie and some of her things. This morning, Mitsuko called me into her room and took me by the arm over to the shrine. "Is this your daughter?" she asked in her halting English as she touched one of the photos. I nodded. She kneeled down, put her hands to prayer position, and bowed deeply.

October 27

Cranky

We drove to Dulles Airport and back today in the rain, and I am cranky. I have a headache; I feel tired and ravenously hungry. I am impatient with talk. I don't want to hear anything about anyone else's life: I have no patience for your problems or your joys. I feel guilty to be so selfish, but I have been hospitable and sociable for a week and I don't have another nice bone in my body.

October 28

Now

I had an epiphany. I have been steeling myself against the impending anniversary of Maggie's death, preparing for a very difficult day. This morning, meditating, I had the thought: *Maggie is not going to die again.* And I know this is crazy, but that was it. Somehow my confused mind was preparing itself for Maggie's death, and for the aftermath. And since then, all day, I have felt lighter.

Over the last few weeks, some sweet plans have evolved: my morning meeting at Daybreak, Mandy's yoga class with Diane, a visit to Maggie's bench with Ruthie. (I know that there is no one whom I can cry with better than Ruthie, who loved Maggie like her own daughter.) Helen and I will go rock climbing in the afternoon, and, in the evening, in another amazing twist of fate, Jim and I will go to hear Blues Traveler at Rams Head with Bill and Terry. I think there's a good balance to the day, and I know I will be okay.

Meg Tipper

October 29

Lunch Outside

It was a gorgeous fall afternoon, the sun lighting up the leaves on the sugar maple in our yard so brilliantly that I had to take a picture of it. Jim's son, Zeke, made us lunch: tomatoes, fresh mozzarella, and my home-made pesto on fresh, hard-crusted, white bread. Heaven. We ate outside at the picnic table, just reveling in the sun and food and enjoying each other's company. I had made the connection to the last time I saw Maggie, our lunch at the picnic table on another beautiful, warm, fall day, how could I not? But I hadn't felt the memory in any fullness.

And then I looked at Zeke and realized powerfully how good it felt to have him there with us; I remembered that I had given Maggie pesto on her noodles and how she had enjoyed them. I remembered the way the sun looked on her hair and the leaves falling into the convertible as I watched Bill and her drive away. Suddenly, I felt so swelled with emotion, passion, really. I can't even name what I was feeling; it was ecstatic, as strong as being in love, as an orgasm. It encompassed love and joy and sorrow and humility. I would have to call it the touch of god.

The greatest irony is that I fought it. I was scared. God

presented itself to me in the splendor of a simple moment and I wanted to hide: take a bite of my sandwich, find something to say. It's okay, but next time, if I am blessed with a next time, I want to better receive the gift.

October 30

Mortal Man

I think of what I have been through this year and am overwhelmed. At the beginning of Barbara Kingsolver's novel, *Animal Dreams*, the father looks at his two daughters, finally sleeping soundly after a near-death accident, and thinks, "God, why does a mortal man have children? It is senseless to love anything this much" (21). My love for both my children is completely senseless: it is instinctive, boundless, visceral. I remember when Bill took Stephen to college, my first child torn away from me, I felt like I had been punched in the gut. I couldn't catch my breath; I was nauseous. Something was missing from my very being. Now, whenever I have a reunion with Stephen, I hold him to me for an extra long time. I want our hearts to beat together for a moment. I feast on him with my eyes.

Later in Kingsolver's book, one of the daughters, Codi, sits with her father as he is dying and realizes that she is "still rooting for his recovery. Pain reaches the heart with electrical speed, but *truth* moves to the heart as slowly as a glacier" (292). Codi and her father are both trained as physicians; they think about the body in medical terms. The pathways of physical pain can be traced, but the journeys of the emotions are mysterious. I know I have been as faithful as I could be to the pain of the loss of Maggie; the truths will be longer coming and more elusive.

October 31

The Pagan New Year

My friend Lucy, who is a much more orthodox pagan than I, tells me that this is the turn of the pagan new year, a time when the divide between the material and spirit worlds is thin. November 2 is All Souls Day in the Catholic Church and The Day of the Dead in South America. It is perhaps no coincidence that Maggie found her way across at this time of year. Both the psychic and the medium said that my father was there at her death to receive and guide her passing. I like thinking of all her angels right there, easily enveloping her: Ganny and Papa, Grandpa Al, Bop, Gummer Ginny, Pop-pop, Nan, Monica, Galen and Arif.

Of course, for children and their parents, this day is Halloween, a holiday Maggie loved. Between dressing up, visiting with friends and neighbors, and getting candy, what was not to like? Maggie went through a phase of several years during which she dressed up as literary figures, which made her English teacher mother especially proud. I remember Heidi, Madeleine, Waldo (from the *Where's Waldo?* books), and Kirsten (from the *American Girl* series). But the Maggie Halloween memory that I treasure most involves her separating all her candy by type and then counting the items in each pile and making a color coded bar graph of her entire Trick or Treat haul! Part of the effort was just the delight of organizing, Maggie having come from two hyper organized parents, but surely the other reason was to inventory her stash to protect against raids from her older brother and her parents. No fool, that girl!

November 1

Every Moment

This is the 365th day.

Stephanie and Chris got married last night; the dress looked beautiful and Stephanie wore my necklace. Part of their ceremony was the promise to "make every moment have meaning." Sometimes I can suffer needlessly because I invest moments with my personal hypersensitivity and give them meaning they don't have, but I know that the spirit of those words was this: Pay attention! Don't miss this life. It is all a gift. We don't even have to make the meaning, just appreciate it.

In the last act of Thornton Wilder's *Our Town*, Emily returns after her death to spend time with her family again, but she is overwhelmed by the intensity of how precious life is and of how much her family is missing. She says to the Stage Manager, "I can't. I can't go on. It goes so fast. We don't have time to look at one another. I didn't realize. So all that was going on and we never noticed" (108).

On my good days, Maggie's death has slowed me down, made me much more attuned, like Emily, to the sweetness of life.

This appreciation of life is one of what my Mom calls

"ripples" from Maggie's life and death, positive impact in every direction. For me, often the effects have seemed more like tsunami waves, but there also have been ripples, and I hope this book will be among them. I hope that reading about the process of my grieving will help others who are grieving to know that they are not crazy and that everything passes. I hope that those who knew Maggie will enjoy my memories and will recall some of their own, and that people who didn't know her will wish they had. Above all, I hope everyone will feel inspired by my amazing daughter to live, give, and love passionately.

Index

Anger: 11.24, 12.1, 3.11, 9.19, 9.23

Bereaved Parents: 11.7, 1.19, 1.22, 2.11, 3.19, 4.6, 4.11, 4.16, 4.20, 4.24, 10.23

Books: 1.28, 6.9, 8.6, 8.20, 9.16, 9.23, 9.29, 10.5

Business: 1.8, 2.9, 5.25, 6.27, 8.26

Comfort: 11.5, 11.11, 11.13, 12.8, 12.26, 3.18, 9.4, 9.18, 10.3

Courage: 12.9, 9.5, 9.29, 10.20

Cycles: 12.15, 1.9, 8.27, 9.9, 9.14, 10.11

Denial: 11.2, 12.5, 2.10, 6.26, 10.17, 10.22

Depression: 1.24, 4.21, 9.10, 9.14

Dreams: 12.17, 1.27, 7.1, 10.2, 10.25

Emotions: 11.9, 11.20, 2.13, 3.4, 3.19, 5.28, 6.28, 7.8, 8.5, 8.10, 8.30, 9.2, 9.8

Energy: 11.21, 11.27, 12.3, 4.5, 5.3, 5.5, 5.21, 6.14, 7.26, 10.1, 10.27

Epilepsy: 11.19, 2.27, 3.14, 4.5, 4.18

Family: 1.14, 2.3, 2.26, 4.15, 5.17, 5.31, 6.24, 7.13, 8.18, 10.8

Fear: 11.26, 6.1, 6.23, 9.30

Friends: 11.15, 12.19, 2.18, 2.24, 3.8, 4.1, 4.2, 4.3, 4.12, 4.14, 5.29, 6.30, 10.4, 10.16

Fundraising: 1.11, 3.5, 7.29, 8.7, 9.22

Gratitude: 1.30, 2.15, 4.4, 5.16, 6.7, 6.15, 8.16, 9.15, 9.19, 10.15

Guilt: 1.10, 2.20, 3.9, 3.29, 4.26, 6.11, 9.11, 9.20, 10.13

Healing: 11.5, 3.15, 3.20, 4.23, 5.6, 7.24, 9.1, 9.22

Jealousy: 6.10, 7.28, 8.28, 10.24

Laughter: 12.21, 6.18, 6.22, 7.10, 9.21, 10.16

Letting go: 11.6, 10.11, 1.12, 3.6, 8.18, 8.23, 8.31, 9.24, 10.7, 10.11, 10.19

Loss: 12.2, 1.25, 2.28, 3.2, 3.10, 3.27, 5.10, 5.18, 6.16, 6.19, 7.31, 8.3, 8.12, 9.6

Love: 11.14, 3.28, 4.8, 5.7, 5.12, 8.29, 10.9, 10.28

Memorials: 11.6, 11.7, 11.8, 11.16, 12.13, 12.14, 12.22, 7.2, 7.12, 9.7

Memories: 11.8, 11.10, 11.12, 12.11, 1.2, 1.4, 1.17, 1.23, 1.29, 2.23, 3.16, 4.5, 4.23, 4.30, 5.8, 5.14, 5.22, 6.6, 6.21, 7.9, 7.18, 7.25, 8.4, 8.15, 8.21, 9.12, 9.25, 10.6, 10.30, 10.31

Mourning: 1.6, 2.16, 3.21, 4.13, 5.4, 5.11, 5.13, 5.23, 6.12, 7.11, 9.13, 9.14, 9.16, 9.20, 9.27

Normal: 12.16, 2.8, 4.17, 4.29, 6.12, 6.13

Pain: 12.4, 2.14, 3.17, 6.20, 9.28

Paradox: 3.1, 3.3, 4.10, 8.14

Physical: 11.4, 12.6, 1.18, 1.21, 2.4, 2.17, 2.22, 5.24, 7.15

Poems: 11.6, 7.6, 10.11, 10.19

Process: 11.3, 12.18, 12.29, 5.15, 5.30, 6.2, 6.5, 7.4, 7.14, 7.16, 7.17, 7.23, 8.2, 8.20, 8.22, 8.25, 9.3, 9.27, 10.28, 11.1

Projects: 11.18, 12.28, 4.9, 6.4, 7.20

Rituals: 12.10, 2.1

Routines: 1.7, 2.5, 2.12, 10.12

Sense of Self: 11.25, 11.30, 12.24, 1.13, 2.19, 2.25, 3.30, 7.7

Serendipity: 11.23, 5.1

Shock: 1.1, 1.3, 1.21, 8.1

Shrine: 1.15, 3.23, 4.25, 7.27

Signs: 12.7, 12.12, 12.23, 1.31, 2.21, 3.24, 3.26, 4.28, 5.2, 5.9, 6.25, 10.10

Spiritual Connections: 11.12, 12.25, 12.27, 12.31, 3.12, 3.13, 3.25, 4.27, 7.3, 8.9

Surrogates: 3.7, 5.27, 6.8, 7.21, 7.22, 8.11, 8.13, 8.19, 10.14

Tears: 12.20, 2.7, 4.19, 5.26, 10.25

Time: 2.1, 3.22, 3.31, 6.3, 6.17, 7.19, 8.24

Twelve Step Recovery: 11.5, 11.27, 12.13, 1.12, 1.13, 2.2, 4.10, 5.6, 5.17, 6.26, 7.14, 8.12, 9.27, 9.28, 10.9, 10.13

Unitarian Universalist: 11.6, 11.16, 4.12, 9.29

Voice: 1.5, 1.16, 6.29

What to Say/Do or What Not to Say/Do: 11.6, 11.7, 11.14, 11.22, 11.28, 12.1, 12.30, 4.7, 4.22, 5.20, 9.17, 10.26

World: 1.20, 10.18, 10.21

Yoga: 3.11, 4.3, 5.26, 6.5, 7.6, 7.7, 7.8, 8.2, 10.12, 10.26

Works Cited

Alcoholics Anonymous. NY: Alcoholics Anonymous World Services, 3rd edition, 1976.

Barnett, Catherine. *Into Perfect Spheres Such Holes are Pierced*. Farmington, ME: Alice James Books, 2004.

Bettelheim, Bruno. *The Uses of Enchantment: The Meaning and Importance of Fairy Tales*. NY: Vintage, 1976.

Bonanno, Kathleen. *Slamming Open the Door*. Farmington, ME: Alice James Books, 2009.

Cameron, Diane. "We are Easter People." *Albany Times Union*. March 31, 2002.

Chodron, Pema. *When Things Fall Apart*. Boston: Shambala Pub. Inc., 1997.

Didion, Joan. *The Year of Magical Thinking*. NY: Knopf, 2005.

Irving, John. *A Widow for One Year*. NY: Random House, 1998.

Fuller, Abigale. "Cultivating Gratitude." *A Journey Together*. Winter, 2009. <http://www.bereavedparentsusa.org/images/Newsletters/v14n1r.pdf>

Garg, Anu. A Word A Day, October 13, 2009. <http://wordsmith.org/awad/>

Gibson, Gregory. *Hubert's Freaks*. <http://hubertsfreaks.com/>

Higgins, Christine. *The Green Door: Ushering Grief*. <http://usheringgrief.blogspot.com>

King, Sorrel. *Josie's Story*. NY: Atlantic, 2009.

Kingsolver, Barbara. *Animal Dreams*. NY: Harper Collins, 1990.

Kubler-Ross, Elizabeth. *On Death and Dying*. NY: Simon &

Schuster, 1969.

Kunitz, Stanley. "The Long Boat." *The Collected Poems*. NY: Norton, 2000.

Lamott, Anne. "Diving into the Wreckage," in *Salon*, July, 1997. <http://www.salon.com/aug97/mothers/lamott970814.html>

Lawson, Mary. *Crow Lake*. NY: Bantam Dell, 2002.

Lehane, Dennis. *Mystic River*. NY: Harper Collins, 2001.

Livingston, Gordon. *Only Spring*. Sydney: Hachette Australia, 1999.

Longfellow, Henry Wadsworth. "The Cross of Snow." Public domain.

Magee, Pilot Officer Gillespie. "High Flight." Public domain.

Martin, Jennifer J. *Star Child*. Lincoln, NE: Iuniverse, 2006.

McEwan, Ian. *Enduring Love*. NY: Nan A. Talese, 1997.

O'Donoghue, John. "For Grief." *To Bless the Space Between Us: A Book of Blessings*. NY: Doubleday, 2008.

"On the Page, Poet Mourns Daughter's Murder." *Fresh Air from WHYY*. July 29, 2009. <http://www.npr.org/templates/story/story.php?storyId=111218053>

O'Rourke, Meghan. "The true nature of mourning." *The Week*. Vol. 9, no. 407. April 10, 2009.

Reader's Digest Complete Guide to Needlework. Pleasantville, NY: The Reader's Digest Association, Inc., 1979.

Rombauer, Irma S. and Marion Rombauer Becker. The Joy of Cooking. Indianapolis, Bobbs-Merrill Company, Inc., 1964.

Setterfield, Diane. *The Thirteenth Tale*. NYC: Washington Square Press, 2006.

Shaffer, Mary Ann & Annie Barrows. *The Guernsey Literary*

and Potato Peel Pie Society. NY: Dial, 2008.

Stoller, Debbie. Stitch 'n Bitch: The Knitter's Handbook. NY: Workman Publishing, 2003.

Weiss, Brian. *Many Lives, Many Masters*. NY: Simon & Schuster, 1988.

Wiggins, Marianne. *Evidence of Things Unseen*. NY: Simon & Shuster, 2003.

Wilder, Thornton. *Our Town*. NY: HarperCollins Perennial Classics Edition, 2003.

Winston, Lolly. *Good Grief.* NY: Warner Books, 2004.

The future of publishing...today!

Apprentice House is the country's only campus-based, student-staffed book publishing company. Directed by professors and industry professionals, it is a nonprofit activity of the Communication Department at Loyola University in Maryland.

Using state-of-the-art technology and an experiential learning model of education, Apprentice House publishes books in untraditional ways. This dual responsibility as publishers and educators creates an unprecedented collaborative environment among faculty and students, while teaching tomorrow's editors, designers, and marketers.

Outside of class, progress on book projects is carried forth by the AH Book Publishing Club, a co-curricular campus organization supported by Loyola University's Office of Student Activities.

Student Project Team for *Standing at the Edge:*
    Jennifer Minich '10

Eclectic and provocative, Apprentice House titles intend to entertain as well as spark dialogue on a variety of topics. Financial contributions to sustain the press's work are welcomed. Contributions are tax deductible to the fullest extent allowed by the IRS.

To learn more about Apprentice House books or to obtain submission guidelines, please visit www.ApprenticeHouse.com.

Apprentice House
Communication Department
Loyola University in Maryland
4501 N. Charles Street
Baltimore, MD 21210
Ph: 410-617-5265 • Fax: 410-617-5040
info@apprenticehouse.com

www.ingramcontent.com/pod-product-compliance
Lightning Source LLC
Chambersburg PA
CBHW070158240426
43671CB00007B/480